JUMB

HEiST

A PERFECT PUZZLE CAPER!

Henri Arnold,
Bob Lee,
David L. Hoyt,
and
Jeff Knurek

TRIUMPH
BOOKS

This book is available in quantity at special discounts
for your group or organization.

For further information, con tact:
Triumph Books LLC
814 North Franklin Street
Chicago, Illinois 60610
Phone: (312) 337-0747
www.triumphbooks.com

Printed in U.S.A.

ISBN: 978-1-63727-46 1-3

Design by Sue Knopf

CONTENTS

JUMBLE®

HEIST

CLASSIC PUZZLES

PUZZLE

1

JUMBLE®

Unscramble these four Jumbles, one letter to each square, to form four ordinary words.

RALNS

MALLA

ROUGAC

INGROI

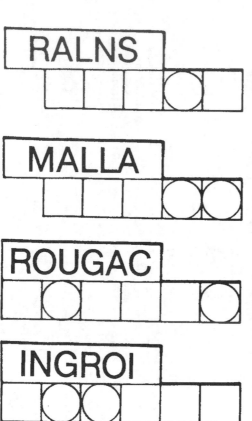

HIGHER TAXES
ACID RAIN
INFLATION
THAT EGOTISTICAL CYNIC SAW NOTHING GOOD IN THE WORLD, WITHOUT THE AID OF THIS.

Now arrange the circled letters to form the surprise answer, as suggested by the above cartoon.

Print answer here

PUZZLE

2

JUMBLE®

Unscramble these four Jumbles, one letter to each square, to form four ordinary words.

DITIO

ZUZYF

KORREB

NAITAT

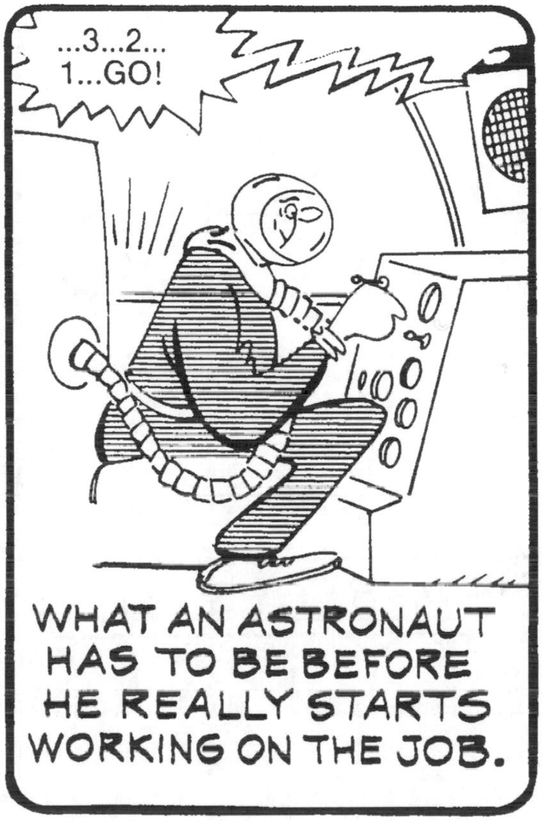
...3...2... 1...GO!
WHAT AN ASTRONAUT HAS TO BE BEFORE HE REALLY STARTS WORKING ON THE JOB.

Now arrange the circled letters to form the surprise answer, as suggested by the above cartoon.

Print answer here " "

PUZZLE

3

JUMBLE®

Unscramble these four Jumbles, one letter to each square, to form four ordinary words.

GALEE

YAMEL

FARIDA

BOTERD

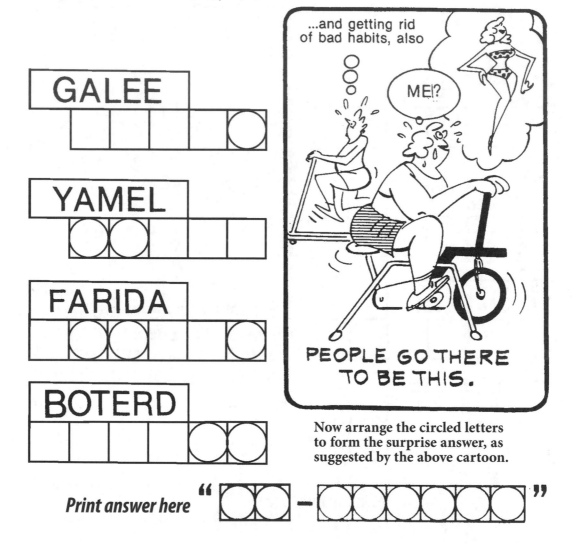

...and getting rid of bad habits, also
ME!?
PEOPLE GO THERE TO BE THIS.

Now arrange the circled letters to form the surprise answer, as suggested by the above cartoon.

Print answer here "◯◯-◯◯◯◯◯◯"

PUZZLE

4

JUMBLE®

Unscramble these four Jumbles, one letter to each square, to form four ordinary words.

PREKO

ESTAE

LAHMYN

YESURT

WHAT THE GAME OF POLO INVOLVES A LOT OF.

Now arrange the circled letters to form the surprise answer, as suggested by the above cartoon.

Print answer here “ ” ”

PUZZLE

5

JUMBLE®

Unscramble these four Jumbles, one letter to each square, to form four ordinary words.

NOICT

MULBA

TYKONT

HIGLES

WHY THEY CALL THEM "TELLERS" AT BANKS.

Now arrange the circled letters to form the surprise answer, as suggested by the above cartoon.

Print answer here ALWAYS " "

PUZZLE

6

JUMBLE®

Unscramble these four Jumbles, one letter to each square, to form four ordinary words.

ENFLO

UCLID

RUSLAW

CHETOL

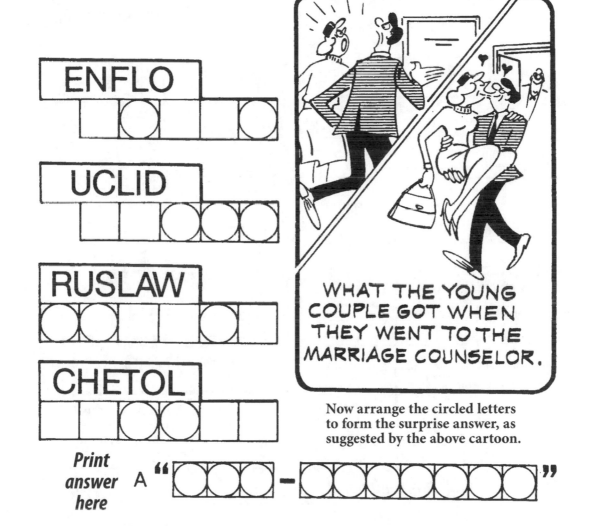

WHAT THE YOUNG COUPLE GOT WHEN THEY WENT TO THE MARRIAGE COUNSELOR.

Now arrange the circled letters to form the surprise answer, as suggested by the above cartoon.

Print answer here A "[ ][ ][ ]-[ ][ ][ ][ ][ ][ ][ ]"

PUZZLE

7

JUMBLE®

Unscramble these four Jumbles, one letter to each square, to form four ordinary words.

OTHIS

PRYAT

TOBUNT

CATHED

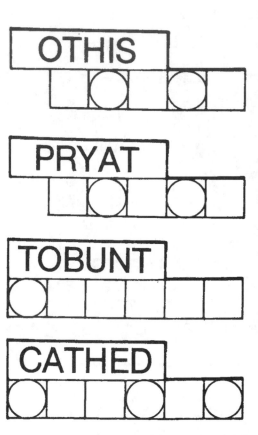

Good idea, Boss, but you're just wasting your time
DIET
HE AIMED TO PLEASE, BUT HE WAS THIS.

Now arrange the circled letters to form the surprise answer, as suggested by the above cartoon.

Print answer here

PUZZLE

8

JUMBLE®

Unscramble these four Jumbles, one letter to each square, to form four ordinary words.

LISKY

NOROH

YORCAN

MUBHEL

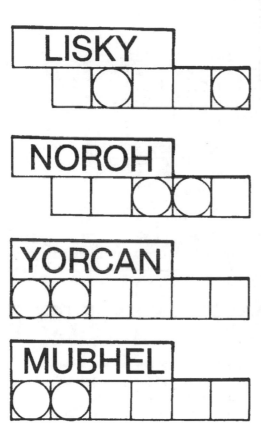

IF YOU WANT TO SUCCEED AS A VIOLINIST, THIS IS HOW YOU HAVE TO GET INVOLVED WITH YOUR MUSIC.

Now arrange the circled letters to form the surprise answer, as suggested by the above cartoon.

Print answer here UP TO

JUMBLE®

Unscramble these four Jumbles, one letter to each square, to form four ordinary words.

VILIC

ETHAB

GROUTH

HILERS

ANOTHER NAME FOR WRITER'S CRAMP.

Now arrange the circled letters to form the surprise answer, as suggested by the above cartoon.

Print answer here " ☐☐☐☐☐☐☐☐☐☐ "

PUZZLE

10

JUMBLE®

Unscramble these four Jumbles, one letter to each square, to form four ordinary words.

TELIE

NUNAL

FLYNUK

LEMPOC

Junior!
HOW HE GOT THE JOB.

Now arrange the circled letters to form the surprise answer, as suggested by the above cartoon.

Print answer here BY "○○○-○○○○○○○"

PUZZLE

11

JUMBLE®

Unscramble these four Jumbles, one letter to each square, to form four ordinary words.

ROWEB

BEPOR

OPTATE

DILFED

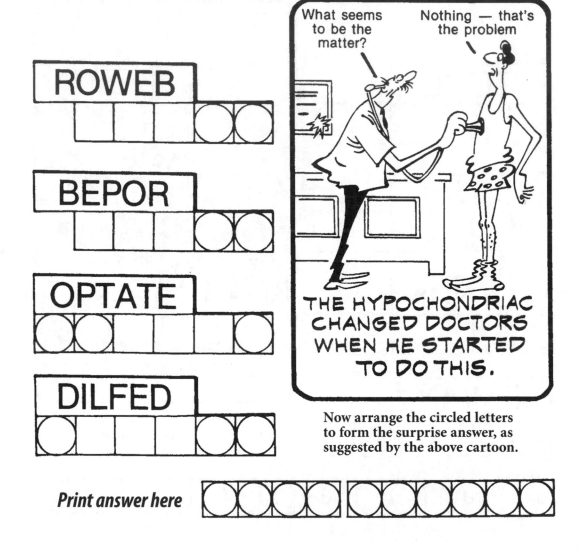

What seems to be the matter?
Nothing — that's the problem
THE HYPOCHONDRIAC CHANGED DOCTORS WHEN HE STARTED TO DO THIS.

Now arrange the circled letters to form the surprise answer, as suggested by the above cartoon.

Print answer here

PUZZLE

12

JUMBLE®

Unscramble these four Jumbles, one letter to each square, to form four ordinary words.

FARCT

LEERD

RAZABA

INFREY

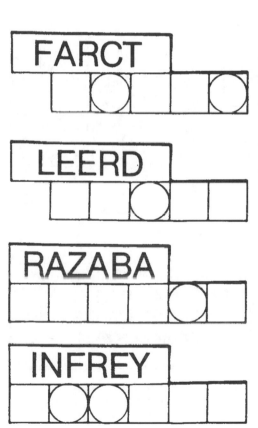

WHAT HE SAID WHEN HE COULDN'T FIND A DECENT PAIR OF SOCKS IN HIS DRAWER.

Now arrange the circled letters to form the surprise answer, as suggested by the above cartoon.

Print answer here " " !

JUMBLE®

Unscramble these four Jumbles, one letter to each square, to form four ordinary words.

TINJO

FORLO

KOTLEC

AVLAND

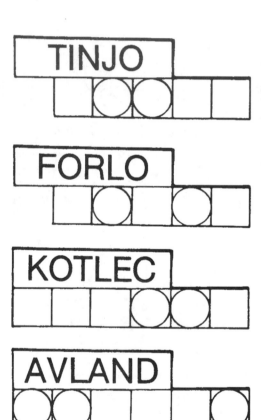

17
8
WHAT THE COACH KEPT SAYING TO THE TEAM OF ZOMBIES.

Now arrange the circled letters to form the surprise answer, as suggested by the above cartoon.

Print answer here !

PUZZLE

14

JUMBLE®

Unscramble these four Jumbles, one letter to each square, to form four ordinary words.

URROF

OBOAT

WADROC

TESKAB

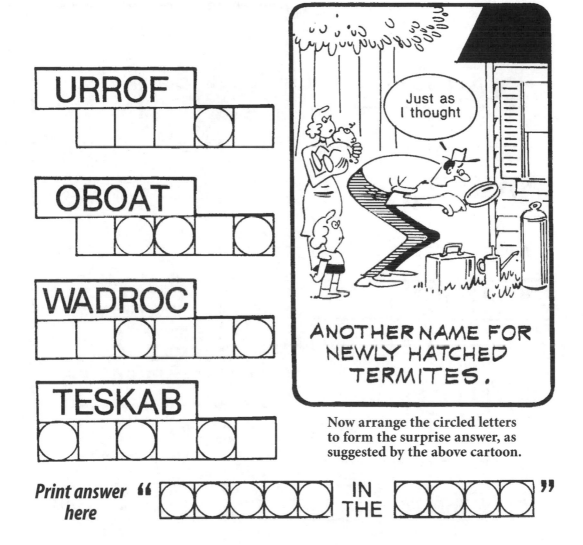

Just as I thought

ANOTHER NAME FOR NEWLY HATCHED TERMITES.

Now arrange the circled letters to form the surprise answer, as suggested by the above cartoon.

Print answer here " ☐☐☐☐☐ IN THE ☐☐☐☐ "

PUZZLE

15

JUMBLE®

Unscramble these four Jumbles, one letter to each square, to form four ordinary words.

DUELE

VENAH

TUSDIP

NAUTER

Such grammar!
THE "TENSE" HE USED MOST FREQUENTLY WHEN MAKING SPEECHES.

Now arrange the circled letters to form the surprise answer, as suggested by the above cartoon.

Print answer here " - "

PUZZLE

16

JUMBLE®

Unscramble these four Jumbles, one letter to each square, to form four ordinary words.

CEPEA

YADIL

FEWURC

KROMES

Now I understand why he's so successful
He's sure got brains
COULD THAT SMART COOKIE BE THIS?

Now arrange the circled letters to form the surprise answer, as suggested by the above cartoon.

Print answer here A ◯◯◯◯ " ◯◯◯◯◯◯◯ "

PUZZLE

17

JUMBLE®

Unscramble these four Jumbles, one letter to each square, to form four ordinary words.

PEINT

GITUL

TRAPIE

BIDROF

WHAT PEOPLE SOMETIMES WERE DURING THE STONE AGE.

Now arrange the circled letters to form the surprise answer, as suggested by the above cartoon.

Print answer here " "

PUZZLE

18

JUMBLE®

Unscramble these four Jumbles, one letter to each square, to form four ordinary words.

LUKKS

DRUIL

RYLAIF

GRENED

They're all too expensive. Let's get out of here

WHAT SHE CALLED HIM WHEN HE WENT BACK ON HIS PROMISE TO BUY HER A MINK.

Now arrange the circled letters to form the surprise answer, as suggested by the above cartoon.

Print answer here

PUZZLE

19

JUMBLE®

Unscramble these four Jumbles, one letter to each square, to form four ordinary words.

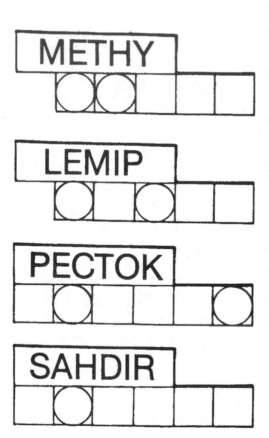

METHY

LEMIP

PECTOK

SAHDIR

I think I dropped that information here
Careful!
MANY A MAN IS BURNED BY PICKING UP THIS.

Now arrange the circled letters to form the surprise answer, as suggested by the above cartoon.

Print answer here

PUZZLE

20

JUMBLE®

Unscramble these four Jumbles, one letter to each square, to form four ordinary words.

HICED

OAKEW

KEDONY

ATWIRE

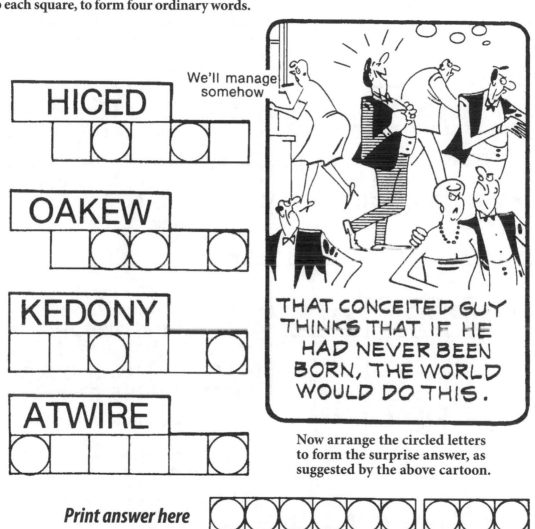

THAT CONCEITED GUY THINKS THAT IF HE HAD NEVER BEEN BORN, THE WORLD WOULD DO THIS.

Now arrange the circled letters to form the surprise answer, as suggested by the above cartoon.

Print answer here

PUZZLE

21

JUMBLE®

Unscramble these four Jumbles, one letter to each square, to form four ordinary words.

PARVO

MUJYP

RUPPEA

LAYREY

Too young to get married
THE BEGINNING OF A DOG'S LIFE MIGHT START WHEN SOMEONE EXPERIENCES THIS.

Now arrange the circled letters to form the surprise answer, as suggested by the above cartoon.

Print answer here

PUZZLE

22

JUMBLE®

Unscramble these four Jumbles, one letter to each square, to form four ordinary words.

GIERT

EVIRT

DOCEED

LARPOR

FOR THAT GAMBLER, THIS WAS THE NEXT THING TO HEAVEN.

Now arrange the circled letters to form the surprise answer, as suggested by the above cartoon.

Print answer here A “_ _ _ _ _ _ _’ _ _ _ _ _”

PUZZLE

23

JUMBLE®

Unscramble these four Jumbles, one letter to each square, to form four ordinary words.

UNMOD

CEWTI

YAWALY

TROPSY

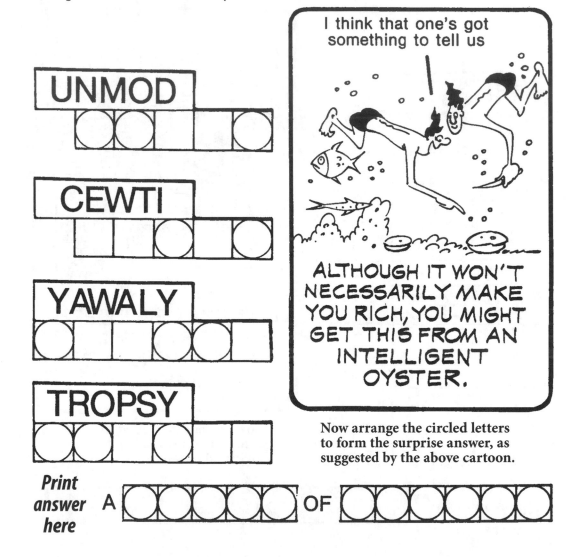

I think that one's got something to tell us

ALTHOUGH IT WON'T NECESSARILY MAKE YOU RICH, YOU MIGHT GET THIS FROM AN INTELLIGENT OYSTER.

Now arrange the circled letters to form the surprise answer, as suggested by the above cartoon.

Print answer here A ◯◯◯◯◯ OF ◯◯◯◯◯◯

PUZZLE

24

JUMBLE®

Unscramble these four Jumbles, one letter to each square, to form four ordinary words.

PHOCE

INGYL

BILDOY

COYTUR

WHAT THE
MOUNTAINEER'S
MASCOT WAS.

Now arrange the circled letters to form the surprise answer, as suggested by the above cartoon.

Print answer here " "

PUZZLE

25

JUMBLE®

Unscramble these four Jumbles, one letter to each square, to form four ordinary words.

CILRY

LYKIM

NESSUL

PERMUB

HOW TO DESCRIBE SOME OF THOSE LATE-NIGHT MOVIES.

Now arrange the circled letters to form the surprise answer, as suggested by the above cartoon.

Print answer here " " OF THE

JUMBLE®

HEIST

DAILY PUZZLES

JUMBLE®

Unscramble these four Jumbles, one letter to each square, to form four ordinary words.

ENZOO

WENYL

URBBUS

TOOWWK

I thought he'd never ask
HE HAD TO GIVE HER A FAKE DIAMOND BECAUSE HE WAS THIS.

Now arrange the circled letters to form the surprise answer, as suggested by the above cartoon.

Print answer here “ ”

PUZZLE

27

JUMBLE®

Unscramble these four Jumbles, one letter to each square, to form four ordinary words.

VALIT

SELOO

LOCHOS

RATTAR

BARGAIN INVESTMENTS
WHAT THE DISCOUNT REAL ESTATE BROKER OFFERED TO SELL.

Now arrange the circled letters to form the surprise answer, as suggested by the above cartoon.

Print answer here "   " FOR

PUZZLE

28

JUMBLE®

Unscramble these four Jumbles, one letter to each square, to form four ordinary words.

NUTED

GEDUN

DIBOLE

ETTORP

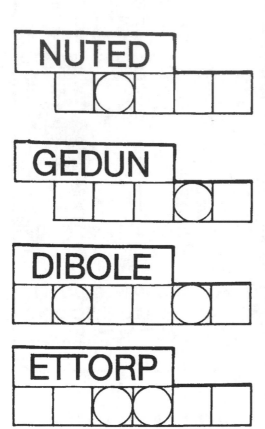

They're all the same
THAT DOOR-TO-DOOR SALESMAN GOT ONLY ONE ORDER---

Now arrange the circled letters to form the surprise answer, as suggested by the above cartoon.

Print answer here " !"

PUZZLE

29

JUMBLE®

Unscramble these four Jumbles, one letter to each square, to form four ordinary words.

RAYRA

KAYWG

BALTOC

DRAWIN

WHAT AN ABSCONDER STEALS AFTER HE STEALS MONEY.

Now arrange the circled letters to form the surprise answer, as suggested by the above cartoon.

Print answer here

PUZZLE

30

JUMBLE®

Unscramble these four Jumbles, one letter to each square, to form four ordinary words.

NOUCE

ROHAB

ENFLOY

AUSANE

HE LAUGHED UP HIS SLEEVE BECAUSE THAT'S WHERE THIS WAS.

Now arrange the circled letters to form the surprise answer, as suggested by the above cartoon.

Print answer here HIS

PUZZLE

31

JUMBLE®

Unscramble these four Jumbles, one letter to each square, to form four ordinary words.

SLEBS

LEHEW

FLOAFY

TEESHE

WHY BUSINESS IS ALWAYS GOOD FOR THE VENDOR OF PEANUTS.

Now arrange the circled letters to form the surprise answer, as suggested by the above cartoon.

Print answer here THEY "   "

PUZZLE

32

JUMBLE®

Unscramble these four Jumbles, one letter to each square, to form four ordinary words.

FLEAB

NOYME

REESHY

HESKLE

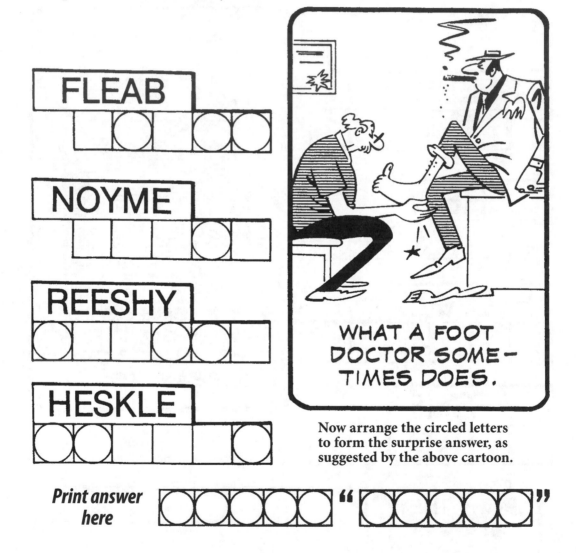

WHAT A FOOT DOCTOR SOME-TIMES DOES.

Now arrange the circled letters to form the surprise answer, as suggested by the above cartoon.

Print answer here “ ”

PUZZLE

33

JUMBLE®

Unscramble these four Jumbles, one letter to each square, to form four ordinary words.

KEVAN

FETHY

NAMMAD

DARNBY

WHAT THAT CANINE PAIR DID WHEN NOAH'S ARK CAME TO THE END OF ITS VOYAGE.

Now arrange the circled letters to form the surprise answer, as suggested by the above cartoon.

Print answer here “ - ”

JUMBLE®

Unscramble these four Jumbles, one letter to each square, to form four ordinary words.

YETID

KAQUE

MIDOWS

NOGALS

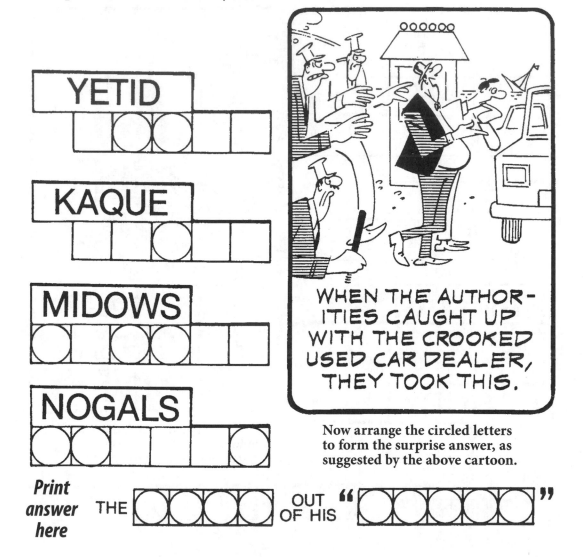

WHEN THE AUTHOR-
ITIES CAUGHT UP
WITH THE CROOKED
USED CAR DEALER,
THEY TOOK THIS.

Now arrange the circled letters to form the surprise answer, as suggested by the above cartoon.

Print answer here THE ◯◯◯◯ OUT OF HIS "◯◯◯◯◯"

PUZZLE

35

JUMBLE®

Unscramble these four Jumbles, one letter to each square, to form four ordinary words.

WADAR

NERTY

ISWUNE

PEWDOL

DOES FISH DISAGREE
WITH YOUR WIFE?

Now arrange the circled letters to form the surprise answer, as suggested by the above cartoon.

Print answer here "IT ______'_ _____!"

PUZZLE

36

JUMBLE®

Unscramble these four Jumbles, one letter to each square, to form four ordinary words.

VEENT

LIQUA

TAIXLY

MASTIG

WHAT THE DIPLOMATS WHO WERE ATTENDING THAT IMPORTANT FUNERAL WERE ALSO DOING.

Now arrange the circled letters to form the surprise answer, as suggested by the above cartoon.

Print answer here " " IN

PUZZLE

37

JUMBLE®

Unscramble these four Jumbles, one letter to each square, to form four ordinary words.

REWFE

HOTOT

CLORLS

PAKRUM

Gosh, I'm sorry

HOW HE FELT WHEN HE FLUNKED THE TELEGRAPHER'S TEST.

Now arrange the circled letters to form the surprise answer, as suggested by the above cartoon.

Print answer here "◯◯-◯◯◯◯◯◯-◯◯◯"

JUMBLE®

Unscramble these four Jumbles, one letter to each square, to form four ordinary words.

LUMPE

KWONN

RATHEH

GIFFEY

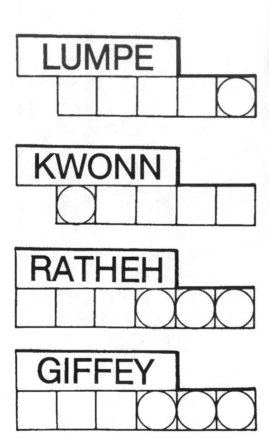

HE WAS ALWAYS "BREAKING INTO" SONG UNTIL HE FOUND THIS.

Now arrange the circled letters to form the surprise answer, as suggested by the above cartoon.

Print answer here THE

PUZZLE

39

JUMBLE®

Unscramble these four Jumbles, one letter to each square, to form four ordinary words.

HILTE

ROARB

NEHBID

GOUTIN

Those outfits cost more than our whole family clothes budget
WHERE ARE SOME OF THOSE YUPPIES RUNNING?

Now arrange the circled letters to form the surprise answer, as suggested by the above cartoon.

Print answer here

PUZZLE

40

JUMBLE®

Unscramble these four Jumbles, one letter to each square, to form four ordinary words.

KEREC

MALUB

YERRSH

DAIMWY

WHAT THE BEE-KEEPER SAID ON AN UNUSUALLY HOT DAY.

Now arrange the circled letters to form the surprise answer, as suggested by the above cartoon.

Print answer here IT'S " "

PUZZLE

41

JUMBLE®

Unscramble these four Jumbles, one letter to each square, to form four ordinary words.

TESED

RAYPH

CHEWEN

FLOUBE

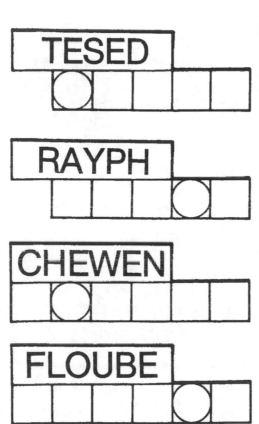

Go ahead -- you deserve a raise
He won't bite you
WHAT THE SIGN ON THE DOOR OF OPPORTUNITY READS.

Now arrange the circled letters to form the surprise answer, as suggested by the above cartoon.

Print answer here " "

PUZZLE

42

JUMBLE®

Unscramble these four Jumbles, one letter to each square, to form four ordinary words.

YAGIL

WHISS

VERGAN

HIPLAC

THEY RESIDED ON THE ROOF BECAUSE THEY LOVED THIS.

Now arrange the circled letters to form the surprise answer, as suggested by the above cartoon.

Print answer here “ ”

PUZZLE

43

JUMBLE®

Unscramble these four Jumbles, one letter to each square, to form four ordinary words.

NAHVE

TALAN

BOALIN

LESTED

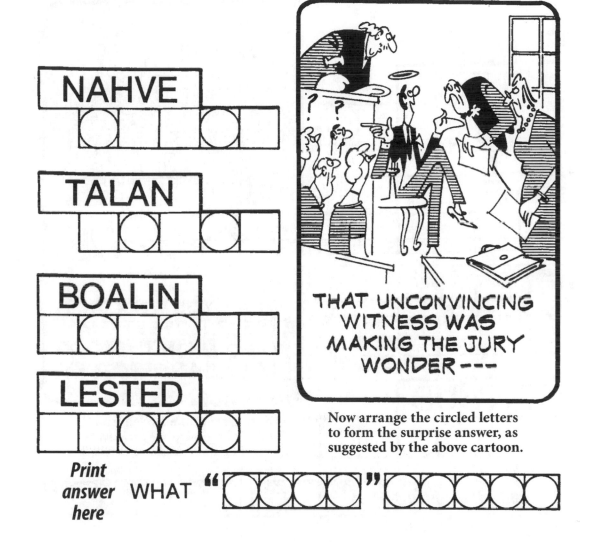

?
?
THAT UNCONVINCING WITNESS WAS MAKING THE JURY WONDER ---

Now arrange the circled letters to form the surprise answer, as suggested by the above cartoon.

Print answer here WHAT " "

PUZZLE

44

JUMBLE®

Unscramble these four Jumbles, one letter to each square, to form four ordinary words.

PLEEO

BELLI

LIFTLE

ENTAUB

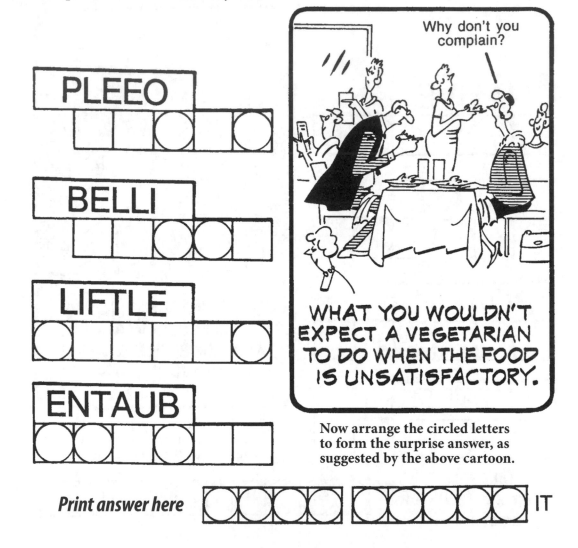

Why don't you complain?
WHAT YOU WOULDN'T EXPECT A VEGETARIAN TO DO WHEN THE FOOD IS UNSATISFACTORY.

Now arrange the circled letters to form the surprise answer, as suggested by the above cartoon.

Print answer here IT

PUZZLE

45

JUMBLE®

Unscramble these four Jumbles, one letter to each square, to form four ordinary words.

PROAN

ORFUR

ULDDEC

CLAMBE

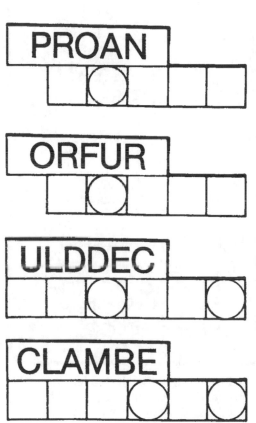

WHAT THAT QUARRELING ACTING TEAM ALWAYS DID JUST BEFORE GOING ON STAGE.

Now arrange the circled letters to form the surprise answer, as suggested by the above cartoon.

Print answer here " "

PUZZLE

46

JUMBLE®

Unscramble these four Jumbles, one letter to each square, to form four ordinary words.

VARFO

NISOB

LOWHYL

GUMMAN

WHAT THAT BASHFUL WALLFLOWER WAS HOPING TO DO WITH THE MAN OF HER CHOICE.

Now arrange the circled letters to form the surprise answer, as suggested by the above cartoon.

Print answer here

PUZZLE

47

JUMBLE®

Unscramble these four Jumbles, one letter to each square, to form four ordinary words.

TALEE

VICLI

MUTTUL

TANIED

COMING SOON!
WHAT A SIESTA IS.

Now arrange the circled letters to form the surprise answer, as suggested by the above cartoon.

Print answer here A ________ "_____"

PUZZLE
48

JUMBLE®

Unscramble these four Jumbles, one letter to each square, to form four ordinary words.

UMPIO

GALOT

HYNDIG

BLATOC

He didn't put a penny in it
It takes money to make money
SHOES
$
$

A GUY WHO TRIES TO START A BUSINESS ON A SHOESTRING SOMETIMES ENDS UP TAKING THIS.

Now arrange the circled letters to form the surprise answer, as suggested by the above cartoon.

Print answer here A ▢▢▢▢ "▢▢▢▢▢▢"

PUZZLE

49

JUMBLE®

Unscramble these four Jumbles, one letter to each square, to form four ordinary words.

TAXEC

RECEL

SAURES

COPILY

THE MOST BRUTAL PART OF THAT HEAVYWEIGHT FIGHT.

Now arrange the circled letters to form the surprise answer, as suggested by the above cartoon.

Print answer here THE ◯◯◯◯◯ OF THE ◯◯◯◯◯

PUZZLE

50

JUMBLE®

Unscramble these four Jumbles, one letter to each square, to form four ordinary words.

NEPEC

LIVIG

TIGBLE

OVVEEL

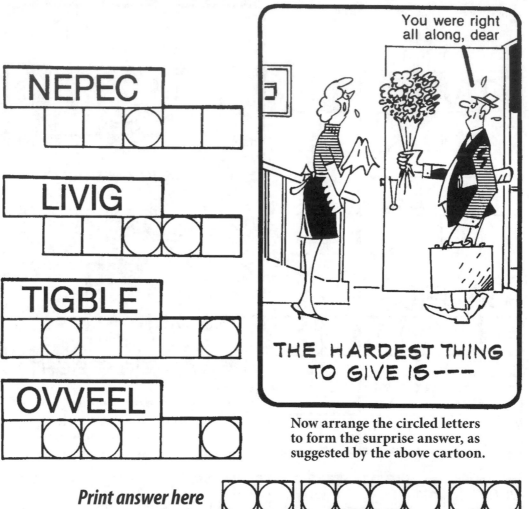

You were right all along, dear
THE HARDEST THING TO GIVE IS---

Now arrange the circled letters to form the surprise answer, as suggested by the above cartoon.

Print answer here

PUZZLE

51

JUMBLE®

Unscramble these four Jumbles, one letter to each square, to form four ordinary words.

DAGEA

REEMY

PEESLY

RUSTEM

WHAT THAT WILD ANIMAL TRAINER AT THE CIRCUS DOES.

Now arrange the circled letters to form the surprise answer, as suggested by the above cartoon.

Print answer here " " TO

PUZZLE

52

JUMBLE®

Unscramble these four Jumbles, one letter to each square, to form four ordinary words.

LITEE

GEDEH

WALLUF

HARTTO

Cheer up -- there are a lot more fish in the sea
I am breaking off our engagement because...
THAT LETTER MADE ILL WILL.

Now arrange the circled letters to form the surprise answer, as suggested by the above cartoon.

Print answer here

PUZZLE

53

JUMBLE®

Unscramble these four Jumbles, one letter to each square, to form four ordinary words.

PRAVO

NOJEY

ADJEGG

HOIBSY

I'm off to gay Paree

WHAT TO SAY WHEN YOUR FRIENDLY SKELETON LEAVES ON VACATION.

Now arrange the circled letters to form the surprise answer, as suggested by the above cartoon.

Print answer here " "

PUZZLE

54

JUMBLE®

Unscramble these four Jumbles, one letter to each square, to form four ordinary words.

YOANN

SHOWE

FOTEEF

TALMED

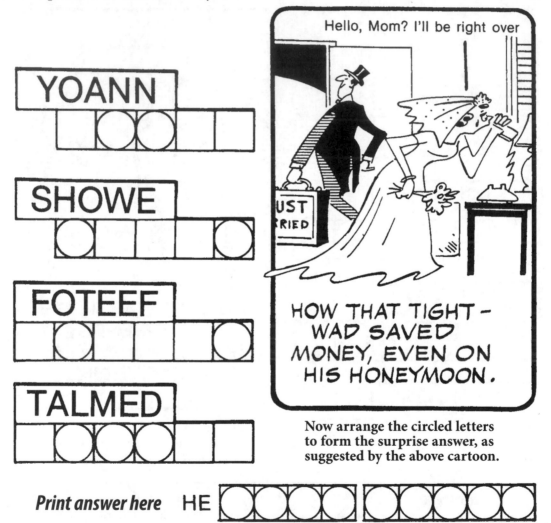

Hello, Mom? I'll be right over
HOW THAT TIGHT-WAD SAVED MONEY, EVEN ON HIS HONEYMOON.

Now arrange the circled letters to form the surprise answer, as suggested by the above cartoon.

Print answer here HE

PUZZLE

55

JUMBLE®

Unscramble these four Jumbles, one letter to each square, to form four ordinary words.

DOREL

NORIM

EDUCAD

LANFIE

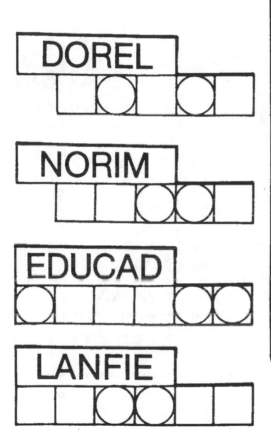

WHAT'S THE BEST DISH TO GET AT A "GREASY SPOON" RESTAURANT?

Now arrange the circled letters to form the surprise answer, as suggested by the above cartoon.

Print answer here

JUMBLE®

Unscramble these four Jumbles, one letter to each square, to form four ordinary words.

TUBOD

RUFIT

MAJEST

HELAGG

Those old sayings get tiresome
WHAT MANY "OLD SAWS" HAVE DONE.

Now arrange the circled letters to form the surprise answer, as suggested by the above cartoon.

Print answer here ◯◯◯◯ THEIR ◯◯◯◯◯

PUZZLE

57

JUMBLE®

Unscramble these four Jumbles, one letter to each square, to form four ordinary words.

SOULE

HEWIG

TESSMY

GIANAU

SOME GUYS ARE WISE, AND SOME ARE THIS.

Now arrange the circled letters to form the surprise answer, as suggested by the above cartoon.

Print answer here “ ”

PUZZLE

58

JUMBLE®

Unscramble these four Jumbles, one letter to each square, to form four ordinary words.

LANUN

BIELL

GIZZAG

RULTSY

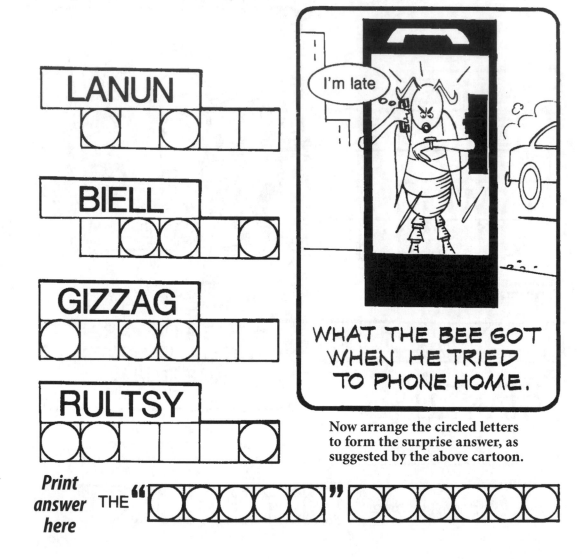

WHAT THE BEE GOT WHEN HE TRIED TO PHONE HOME.

Now arrange the circled letters to form the surprise answer, as suggested by the above cartoon.

Print answer here THE "   "

PUZZLE

59

JUMBLE®

Unscramble these four Jumbles, one letter to each square, to form four ordinary words.

CHULG

HIDUM

REZIFE

LESING

She sounds better than ever
THE SOPRANO STOOD ON THE BALCONY SO SHE COULD DO THIS.

Now arrange the circled letters to form the surprise answer, as suggested by the above cartoon.

Print answer here “ ”

PUZZLE

60

JUMBLE®

Unscramble these four Jumbles, one letter to each square, to form four ordinary words.

TYFFI

PROUG

GININN

RIVFEY

Now arrange the circled letters to form the surprise answer, as suggested by the above cartoon.

Print answer here " ___ ______ "

PUZZLE

61

JUMBLE®

Unscramble these four Jumbles, one letter to each square, to form four ordinary words.

MOCTE

TULGI

NUDEAS

FACEEF

WHAT HE FINALLY LEARNED HOW TO DO WHILE LYING ON THE PSYCHIATRIST'S COUCH.

Now arrange the circled letters to form the surprise answer, as suggested by the above cartoon.

Print answer here ON HIS OWN

PUZZLE

62

JUMBLE®

Unscramble these four Jumbles, one letter to each square, to form four ordinary words.

SILAA

MEERB

CELLOA

KLUSCE

HOW MUCH DID A BELT USED TO COST?

Now arrange the circled letters to form the surprise answer, as suggested by the above cartoon.

Print answer here ☐☐☐☐ THAN A "☐☐☐☐☐-☐☐"

PUZZLE

63

JUMBLE®

Unscramble these four Jumbles, one letter to each square, to form four ordinary words.

LEZBA

ALCKO

NAULCY

CAPTEK

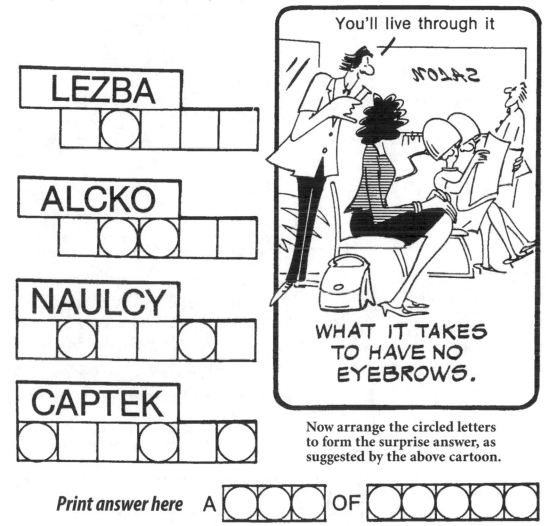

You'll live through it
SALON

WHAT IT TAKES TO HAVE NO EYEBROWS.

Now arrange the circled letters to form the surprise answer, as suggested by the above cartoon.

Print answer here A ___ OF _____

PUZZLE

64

JUMBLE®

Unscramble these four Jumbles, one letter to each square, to form four ordinary words.

PYTEM

SIADY

COBDIE

RILIVE

THEIR RELATIVE WHO WAS KNOWN FOR HIS STINGINESS MUST HAVE BEEN THIS.

Now arrange the circled letters to form the surprise answer, as suggested by the above cartoon.

Print answer here “ ”

PUZZLE

65

JUMBLE®

Unscramble these four Jumbles, one letter to each square, to form four ordinary words.

DUWNE

YEASS

BARJEB

ANTUSE

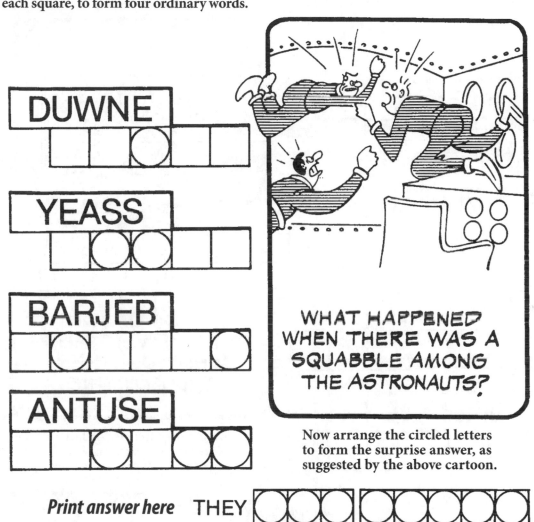

WHAT HAPPENED WHEN THERE WAS A SQUABBLE AMONG THE ASTRONAUTS?

Now arrange the circled letters to form the surprise answer, as suggested by the above cartoon.

Print answer here THEY

PUZZLE

66

JUMBLE®

Unscramble these four Jumbles, one letter to each square, to form four ordinary words.

ROJEK

DYNOW

ARCOWD

NAHZIG

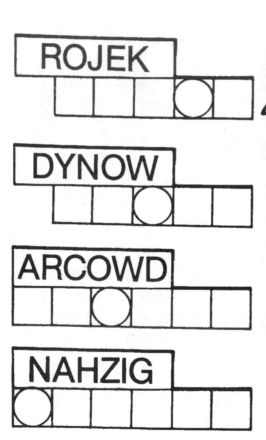

THE GOSSIP WAS PUTTING "WHO" AND "WHO" TOGETHER AND GOT THIS.

Now arrange the circled letters to form the surprise answer, as suggested by the above cartoon.

Print answer here " !"

PUZZLE

67

JUMBLE®

Unscramble these four Jumbles, one letter to each square, to form four ordinary words.

AGGUE

CLEAB

BURGYB

GYABIM

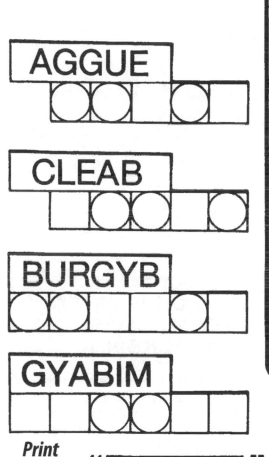

We stopped at all the most expensive hotels, and...
WHAT THOSE BIG-SPENDING TOURISTS RETURNED WITH.

Now arrange the circled letters to form the surprise answer, as suggested by the above cartoon.

Print answer here " ◯◯◯◯ " & ◯◯◯◯◯◯◯◯

PUZZLE

68

JUMBLE®

Unscramble these four Jumbles, one letter to each square, to form four ordinary words.

BYBOH

DARNB

MIRBLE

HETTER

SHAKESPEARE
MILTON
PLATO
BIBLE
WHAT THAT FAMOUS WRITER FOUND MOST ABSORBING.

Now arrange the circled letters to form the surprise answer, as suggested by the above cartoon.

Print answer here

PUZZLE

69

JUMBLE®

Unscramble these four Jumbles, one letter to each square, to form four ordinary words.

LEXIE

NAHDY

PRELIF

TICPED

WHAT THOSE STONE AGE PEOPLE BECAME WHEN THAT PREHIS- TORIC MONSTER SUDDENLY APPEARED OUT OF NOWHERE.

Now arrange the circled letters to form the surprise answer, as suggested by the above cartoon.

Print answer here " "

PUZZLE

70

JUMBLE®

Unscramble these four Jumbles, one letter to each square, to form four ordinary words.

HOWSY

NAGGI

WRAITE

DEHEAB

WHAT THAT GUM-CHEWING GAMBLER LOST.

Now arrange the circled letters to form the surprise answer, as suggested by the above cartoon.

Print answer here

PUZZLE

71

JUMBLE®

Unscramble these four Jumbles, one letter to each square, to form four ordinary words.

ELZAH

LAWRD

CROFIL

TEFNIC

See? I told you so
WHAT WAS THE STORY ABOUT THE DOG THAT CHASED THE STICK FOR TWO MILES?

Now arrange the circled letters to form the surprise answer, as suggested by the above cartoon.

Print answer here " "

PUZZLE

72

JUMBLE®

Unscramble these four Jumbles, one letter to each square, to form four ordinary words.

KEVOE

TUMON

SWEENT

UFTOIT

WHAT KIND OF MUSIC DID THE FIDDLER'S SQUEAKING SHOES MAKE?

Now arrange the circled letters to form the surprise answer, as suggested by the above cartoon.

Print answer here " "

PUZZLE

73

JUMBLE®

Unscramble these four Jumbles, one letter to each square, to form four ordinary words.

BRILO

CENOU

MEBBUN

RUSTYD

THE KANGAROO PROVED TO BE A VALUABLE MEMBER OF THE FOOT-BALL TEAM BECAUSE HE WAS NEVER THIS.

Now arrange the circled letters to form the surprise answer, as suggested by the above cartoon.

Print answer here OF

PUZZLE

74

JUMBLE®

Unscramble these four Jumbles, one letter to each square, to form four ordinary words.

HARAJ

SIVOR

KLANTE

GODINI

PROVIDES THE MAIN COURSE ON A FLIGHT.

Now arrange the circled letters to form the surprise answer, as suggested by the above cartoon.

Print answer here THE

PUZZLE

75

JUMBLE®

Unscramble these four Jumbles, one letter to each square, to form four ordinary words.

FRADT

EAPEY

LUFOWE

DARCCO

THE SWIMMING POOL WAS MORE THAN HE COULD AFFORD, AND NOW HE'S---

Now arrange the circled letters to form the surprise answer, as suggested by the above cartoon.

Print answer here IN

PUZZLE

76

JUMBLE®

Unscramble these four Jumbles, one letter to each square, to form four ordinary words.

BROEP

VELED

INJOAD

TUMONT

Whew! That does it
SHE'LL NO LONGER STAND FOR BEING PAINTED.

Now arrange the circled letters to form the surprise answer, as suggested by the above cartoon.

Print answer here A

PUZZLE

77

JUMBLE®

Unscramble these four Jumbles, one letter to each square, to form four ordinary words.

LOUFT

DULEE

SORABB

PAWNEO

Health Club
THE BEST PLACE TO KEEP YOUR WEIGHT DOWN.

Now arrange the circled letters to form the surprise answer, as suggested by the above cartoon.

Print answer here ______ THE ____

PUZZLE

78

JUMBLE®

Unscramble these four Jumbles, one letter to each square, to form four ordinary words.

TAGUM

KELLN

NECTED

ENLOUG

WHAT WORD FORMED IN HIS MIND FROM CONTEMPLATING THAT "NEAT LEG"?

Now arrange the circled letters to form the surprise answer, as suggested by the above cartoon.

Print answer here " "

PUZZLE

79

JUMBLE®

Unscramble these four Jumbles, one letter to each square, to form four ordinary words.

KAHIK

GORPY

YOJECK

DAWTOR

WHAT KIDS NEVER PLAY IN SCHOOL.

Now arrange the circled letters to form the surprise answer, as suggested by the above cartoon.

Print answer here

PUZZLE

80

JUMBLE®

Unscramble these four Jumbles, one letter to each square, to form four ordinary words.

LUGBY

HEANN

DUBACT

NEURED

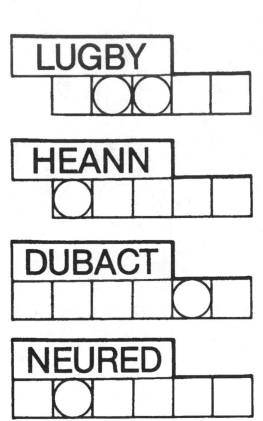

VERY COMMONLY CAUSES WORK STOPPAGES.

Now arrange the circled letters to form the surprise answer, as suggested by the above cartoon.

Print answer here

JUMBLE®

Unscramble these four Jumbles, one letter to each square, to form four ordinary words.

ZOWYO

SLOAS

LXAHEE

BRRAOH

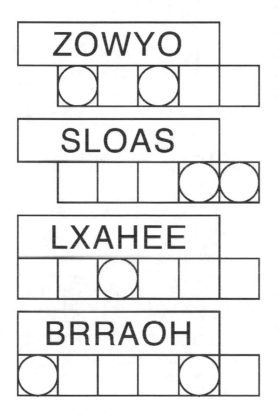

Which owl said that?
I can't tell. What did they say?
WITH SO MANY OWLS IN THE SAME PLACE, IT WAS HARD TO TELL ---

Now arrange the circled letters to form the surprise answer, as suggested by the above cartoon.

Print answer here ___ ' _ " ___ "

PUZZLE

82

JUMBLE®

Unscramble these four Jumbles, one letter to each square, to form four ordinary words.

MUYRM

NTLUB

NISRPG

SSUECN

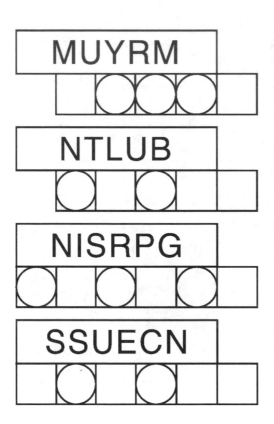

Now, we're going to add these together.
1+2=
2+3=
4+2+1=
1+2+3+4=
I'm totally lost.
TO TEACH ADDITION TO THE STUDENTS, THE TEACHER WROTE ---

Now arrange the circled letters to form the surprise answer, as suggested by the above cartoon.

Print answer here " "

PUZZLE

83

JUMBLE®

Unscramble these four Jumbles, one letter to each square, to form four ordinary words.

YAWER

LKAEN

DOUFEN

HGRIFT

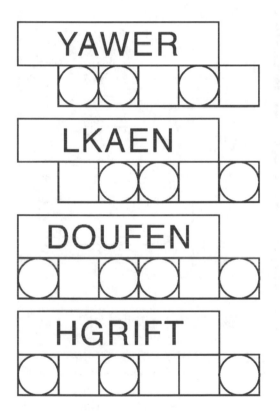

I'm off to piano lessons.
I'm off to Spanish tutoring.
No. You're going to Spanish and you're going to piano. You're not fooling me.

PEOPLE THOUGHT THE TWINS WERE IDENTICAL, BUT THEIR MOM ---

Now arrange the circled letters to form the surprise answer, as suggested by the above cartoon.

Print answer here

PUZZLE

84

JUMBLE®

Unscramble these four Jumbles, one letter to each square, to form four ordinary words.

SOEEB

GYECA

UROCKN

SDOYTG

Wouldn't it be nice if you all got along? When will you grow up?
Isn't this fun, fun, fun?
Do it again!
I'll get around to getting you back!

WHEN BRIAN, DENNIS AND CARL WILSON ROUGHHOUSED ON THE BEACH, THEY WERE BEING ---

Now arrange the circled letters to form the surprise answer, as suggested by the above cartoon.

Print answer here " _ _ _ _ - _ _ _ _ _ _ "

PUZZLE

85

JUMBLE®

Unscramble these four Jumbles, one letter to each square, to form four ordinary words.

ONZEO

KNASC

NAUTBE

UOESDX

You're always going to follow me.
You're nothing compared to me. You're just my opening act.
What's that make me?
THE FIRST POSITIVE NUMBER HAD A BIG EGO AND WAS PROUD TO BE ---

Now arrange the circled letters to form the surprise answer, as suggested by the above cartoon.

Print answer here

PUZZLE

86

JUMBLE®

Unscramble these four Jumbles, one letter to each square, to form four ordinary words.

VOEMI

IMLTI

MEDATN

TAULNW

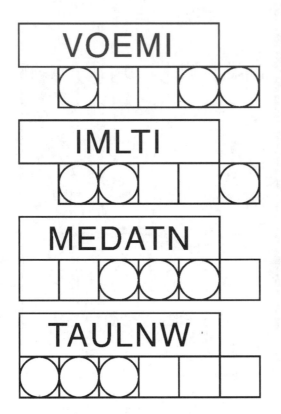

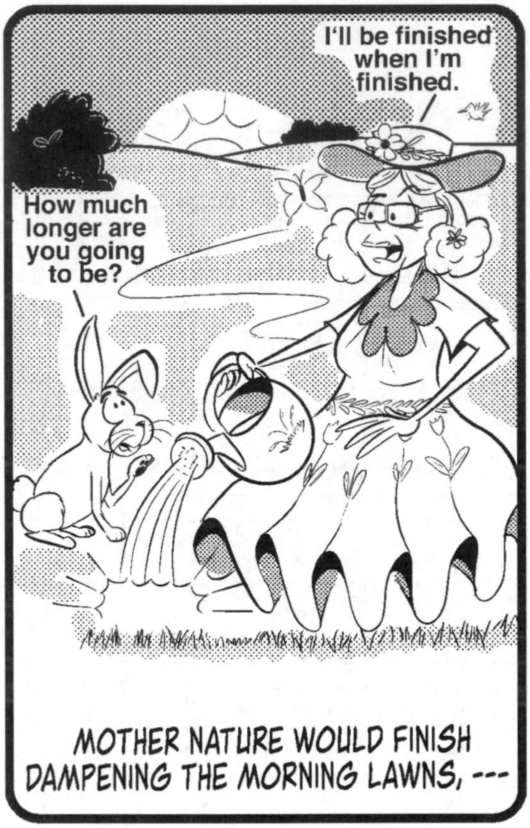

I'll be finished when I'm finished.
How much longer are you going to be?
MOTHER NATURE WOULD FINISH DAMPENING THE MORNING LAWNS, ---

Now arrange the circled letters to form the surprise answer, as suggested by the above cartoon.

Print answer here

" "

JUMBLE®

Unscramble these four Jumbles, one letter to each square, to form four ordinary words.

HMUTP

LOICC

SINWUE

CATEPK

I'm sorry, I only have one seat up front.
Check again!
Don't worry. I'm fine in the back.

WHEN THERE WEREN'T ENOUGH BUSINESS-CLASS SEATS, THE BASEBALL PLAYER SAID ---

Now arrange the circled letters to form the surprise answer, as suggested by the above cartoon.

Print answer here

PUZZLE

88

JUMBLE®

Unscramble these four Jumbles, one letter to each square, to form four ordinary words.

CCMIO

NHKUC

WPASYM

PEUDXL

We are getting these for dessert. Save some room.
Hey! Stop eating them all!
THEY WERE CAREFULLY SELECTING WHICH BERRIES TO EAT. IT WAS FUN TO ---

Now arrange the circled letters to form the surprise answer, as suggested by the above cartoon.

Print answer here

PUZZLE

89

JUMBLE®

Unscramble these four Jumbles, one letter to each square, to form four ordinary words.

CUENL

RSOCS

NETYDR

LLAOEC

Any word on sticking around?
We have our room and tee times for two more days!
THE GOLFERS AT ST. ANDREWS DECIDED TO EXTEND THEIR TRIP SO THEY COULD ---

Now arrange the circled letters to form the surprise answer, as suggested by the above cartoon.

Print answer here ◯◯◯◯ THE ◯◯◯◯◯◯

PUZZLE

90

JUMBLE®

Unscramble these four Jumbles, one letter to each square, to form four ordinary words.

NLBDA

UDOAI

HYOTTO

GIPOST

That shirt still looks great!
I hand wash it and line dry it. It still rocks!
U2
HE BOUGHT THE SHIRT AT THE CONCERT 30 YEARS AGO. TO HIM IT WAS AN --

Now arrange the circled letters to form the surprise answer, as suggested by the above cartoon.

Print answer here "_ _ _-_" _ _ _ _ "_ _ _ _ _-_"

PUZZLE

91

JUMBLE®

Unscramble these four Jumbles, one letter to each square, to form four ordinary words.

VAHYE

ICIMM

MLYHAN

DUTBEG

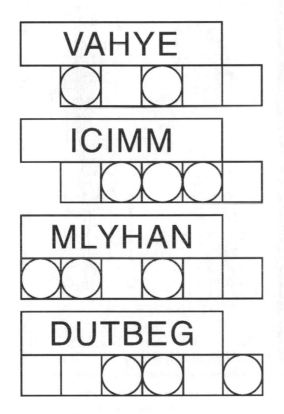

Hola, bonjour, guten Tag, greetings.
Very impressive, your majesty.
Look at him up there!
He's so full of himself.
THE ARROGANT KING WHO COULD SAY "HELLO" IN MANY LANGUAGES WAS ---

Now arrange the circled letters to form the surprise answer, as suggested by the above cartoon.

Print answer here " ◯◯ " ◯◯◯ ◯◯◯◯◯◯

PUZZLE

92

JUMBLE®

Unscramble these four Jumbles, one letter to each square, to form four ordinary words.

SFINF

UGYBG

TRECIM

BFAULI

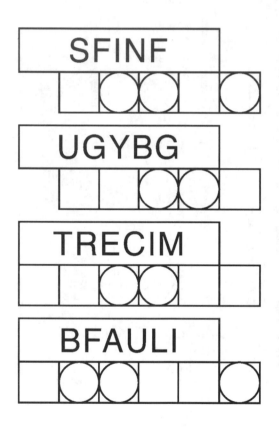

Wow, John! You did it! You must be so happy!
How could you tell?
IT TOOK HIM A YEAR TO LOSE 100 POUNDS, WHICH RESULTED IN A ---

Now arrange the circled letters to form the surprise answer, as suggested by the above cartoon.

Print answer here

PUZZLE

93

JUMBLE®

Unscramble these four Jumbles, one letter to each square, to form four ordinary words.

VORRE

EDAAH

CCHEIT

MOCNIE

Now arrange the circled letters to form the surprise answer, as suggested by the above cartoon.

Print answer here “ ” “ ”

PUZZLE

94

JUMBLE®

Unscramble these four Jumbles, one letter to each square, to form four ordinary words.

DUNEP

NOONI

BHPAUC

TDOMEH

Fido's Famous Bone Bites
We have a winner! Who's a good boy? Scout is!
THE WINNER OF THE DOG BONE EATING CONTEST WAS THE ---

Now arrange the circled letters to form the surprise answer, as suggested by the above cartoon.

Print answer here " ◯◯◯◯◯◯◯◯ "

PUZZLE

95

JUMBLE®

Unscramble these four Jumbles, one letter to each square, to form four ordinary words.

METTP

GRTIE

OAHLPO

SOLONE

Now arrange the circled letters to form the surprise answer, as suggested by the above cartoon.

Print answer here

PUZZLE

96

JUMBLE®

Unscramble these four Jumbles, one letter to each square, to form four ordinary words.

LEPSL

SYATT

BEUUSD

RYWENI

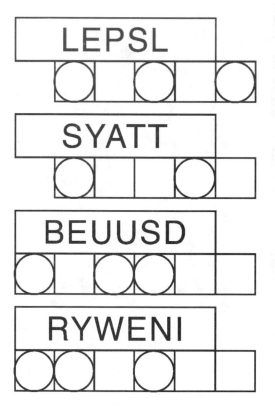

THE SCUBA DIVERS GOT MARRIED UNDERWATER AND BEGAN THEIR NEW LIFE TOGETHER IN ---

Now arrange the circled letters to form the surprise answer, as suggested by the above cartoon.

Print answer here " "

PUZZLE

97

JUMBLE®

Unscramble these four Jumbles, one letter to each square, to form four ordinary words.

NTEIP

DEIUG

TEROBT

WORDAT

DAILY PLANET
I need you to drop everything and cover the story from the mayor's press conference for the front page tomorrow.
Will do!
IF THE NEWSPAPER REPORTER WAS GOING TO TURN IN THE STORY IN TIME, HE'D NEED TO ---

Now arrange the circled letters to form the surprise answer, as suggested by the above cartoon.

Print answer here ◯◯◯ "◯◯◯◯◯" ◯◯ ◯◯

PUZZLE

98

JUMBLE®

Unscramble these four Jumbles, one letter to each square, to form four ordinary words.

KEYRP

NGIRW

GNOREL

NTOAAS

WHEN THE TENNIS PLAYERS TALKED BUSINESS DURING THEIR MATCH, THEY WERE ---

Now arrange the circled letters to form the surprise answer, as suggested by the above cartoon.

Print answer here

PUZZLE

99

JUMBLE®

Unscramble these four Jumbles, one letter to each square, to form four ordinary words.

HIGET

VORCE

SNARKH

APTINC

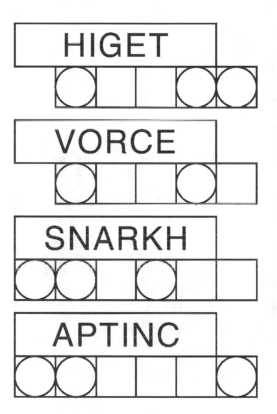

Well, hello! Where are you going, little one?
I'm out of here!

WHEN THE CHICK WAS READY TO LEAVE ITS SHELL, IT TOOK THE ---

Now arrange the circled letters to form the surprise answer, as suggested by the above cartoon.

Print answer here

PUZZLE

100

JUMBLE®

Unscramble these four Jumbles, one letter to each square, to form four ordinary words.

COLLA

GREEM

NPURSG

BLINEB

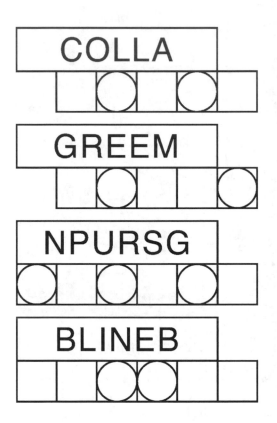

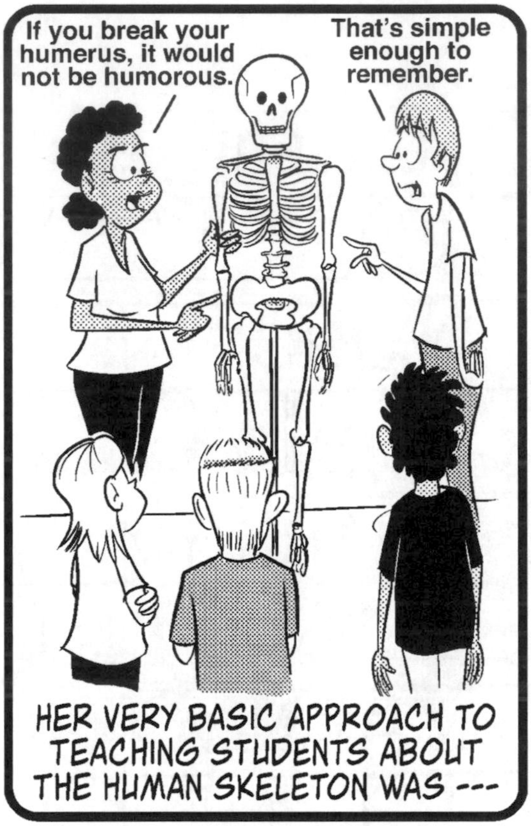

If you break your humerus, it would not be humorous.
That's simple enough to remember.
HER VERY BASIC APPROACH TO TEACHING STUDENTS ABOUT THE HUMAN SKELETON WAS ---

Now arrange the circled letters to form the surprise answer, as suggested by the above cartoon.

Print answer here

PUZZLE

101

JUMBLE®

Unscramble these four Jumbles, one letter to each square, to form four ordinary words.

LIEPX

IRRVE

SEFWET

NTFNAO

I'm sorry. I only saw him from the side.
We should be able to find him from this.
I'll put an APB out for him.

THEY HAD THE POLICE ARTIST'S SILHOUETTE SKETCH AND LOOKED FOR SOMEONE WHO ---

Now arrange the circled letters to form the surprise answer, as suggested by the above cartoon.

Print answer here ☐☐☐ **THE** ☐☐☐☐☐☐☐

PUZZLE

102

JUMBLE®

Unscramble these four Jumbles, one letter to each square, to form four ordinary words.

FJYIF

TUHMO

OIRRRM

CRUPES

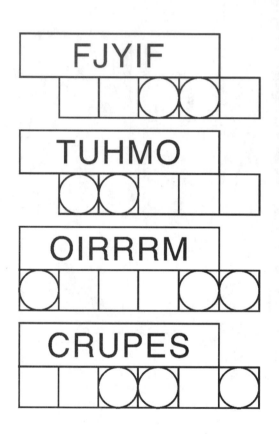

Welcome! We hope you all enjoy your new space!
This is the place to be.
Wow! Impressive!
I bet they'll raise our taxes now.

ANCIENT ROMANS WANTED A LARGE PUBLIC SQUARE, SO THEY BUILT A ---

Now arrange the circled letters to form the surprise answer, as suggested by the above cartoon.

Print answer here

PUZZLE

103

JUMBLE®

Unscramble these four Jumbles, one letter to each square, to form four ordinary words.

CUHNM

ECAPE

GHALEG

RAAATV

Let's see how the Giants are doing.
Two clicks! Not a problem.
Then back to the Lions.
CLICK
FOR SPORTS FANS, THE INVENTION OF THE REMOTE CONTROL WAS A ---

Now arrange the circled letters to form the surprise answer, as suggested by the above cartoon.

Print answer here

PUZZLE

104

JUMBLE®

Unscramble these four Jumbles, one letter to each square, to form four ordinary words.

CRILY

SEYMS

XTROVE

TANUMU

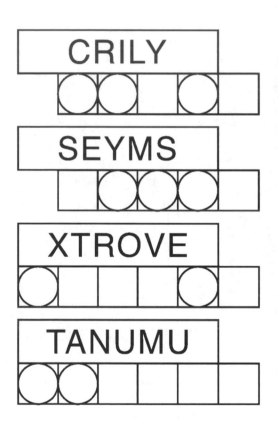

How did you come up with such an idea?
I thought if I could capture the focal points on two pieces of glass, I could see both far and close.

BEN FRANKLIN WAS ABLE TO INVENT BIFOCALS BECAUSE OF HIS ABILITY TO ---

Now arrange the circled letters to form the surprise answer, as suggested by the above cartoon.

Print answer here " - "

PUZZLE

105

JUMBLE®

Unscramble these four Jumbles, one letter to each square, to form four ordinary words.

ONGIG

GOYFG

BRUYGB

UUTFER

I'll get the flea shampoo.
Looks like someone needs a bath.
Leave me alone!
THE DOG WITH THE FLEA PROBLEM TOLD THE SMALL PARASITIC INSECTS TO ---

Now arrange the circled letters to form the surprise answer, as suggested by the above cartoon.

Print answer here

PUZZLE

106

JUMBLE®

Unscramble these four Jumbles, one letter to each square, to form four ordinary words.

LORED

CKONK

SLOFIS

ECCTAN

He is odd.
Yep.
Think about it. Multiply yourselves with me and you're you. I'm a pretty big deal.
You're so full of yourself!
I'm three times the number of you!

THE FIRST POSITIVE ODD NUMBER CONSIDERED ITSELF TO BE ---

Now arrange the circled letters to form the surprise answer, as suggested by the above cartoon.

Print answer here

PUZZLE

107

JUMBLE®

Unscramble these four Jumbles, one letter to each square, to form four ordinary words.

BEAVO

SSIWH

PLEETL

RDTUYS

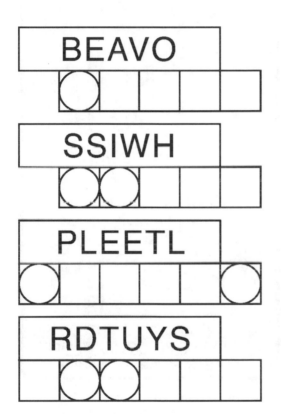

How could our power usage triple in just one month?
Why are all the lights off?
SHE CALLED ABOUT HER UNUSUALLY HIGH ELECTRIC BILL AND ASKED ---

Now arrange the circled letters to form the surprise answer, as suggested by the above cartoon.

Print answer here “ ” ?

PUZZLE

108

JUMBLE®

Unscramble these four Jumbles, one letter to each square, to form four ordinary words.

IGIDT

FIDTR

MEETXP

COEJTB

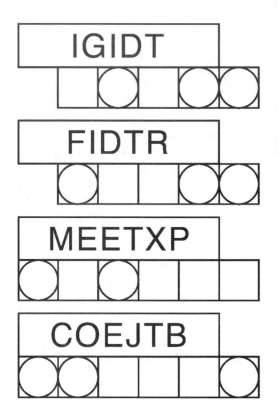

What's going on? I can hear you grumbling in the other room.
I want to look sharp, but I can't find anything!
GETTING READY TO PUT ON HIS BEST SUIT, HE COULDN'T FIND HIS NECKWEAR. HE WAS ---

Now arrange the circled letters to form the surprise answer, as suggested by the above cartoon.

Print answer here

PUZZLE

109

JUMBLE®

Unscramble these four Jumbles, one letter to each square, to form four ordinary words.

HUGLC

LETNK

TTEEIP

WABEER

Here it comes! We've got water!
Yes! I'll let the town know!
Boy did we all need this!
THEY SUCCESSFULLY DRILLED FOR WATER, AND IT HELPED WITH EVERYONE'S ---

Now arrange the circled letters to form the surprise answer, as suggested by the above cartoon.

Print answer here

PUZZLE

110

JUMBLE®

Unscramble these four Jumbles, one letter to each square, to form four ordinary words.

CWIET

DENKE

TYOERH

MRUNEB

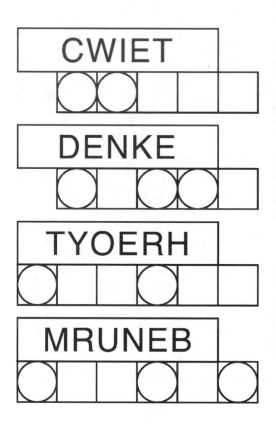

You all better run away from this. I'm all in!
That sounds familiar.
You said that exact thing last time you were bluffing!
THEIR POKER BUDDY TRIED TO BLUFF, BUT THEY ---

Now arrange the circled letters to form the surprise answer, as suggested by the above cartoon.

Print answer here “ ”

PUZZLE

111

JUMBLE®

Unscramble these four Jumbles, one letter to each square, to form four ordinary words.

TINYU

IGBEE

DLIFED

GTYIZL

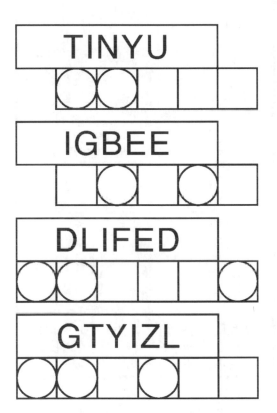

What's wrong? Are you OK?
I think the chicken wasn't cooked enough.
HE HAD NO PROOF THAT THE FOOD WAS GIVING HIM INDIGESTION, BUT HE DID HAVE A ---

Now arrange the circled letters to form the surprise answer, as suggested by the above cartoon.

Print answer here

PUZZLE

112

JUMBLE®

Unscramble these four Jumbles, one letter to each square, to form four ordinary words.

AGEMO

NOYRI

GROJEG

COIYID

I can't put it down!
Isn't it wonderful?
I was so happy to get my hands on "Ulysses"!
ULYSSES
It really is his best work yet!

JAMES WROTE NOVELS SUCH AS "DUBLINERS" AND "ULYSSES," AND HIS READERS ---

Now arrange the circled letters to form the surprise answer, as suggested by the above cartoon.

Print answer here " ◯◯ - ◯◯◯◯◯◯ "

PUZZLE

113

JUMBLE®

Unscramble these four Jumbles, one letter to each square, to form four ordinary words.

NGLUC

RAHDO

CLIPES

GIKSIN

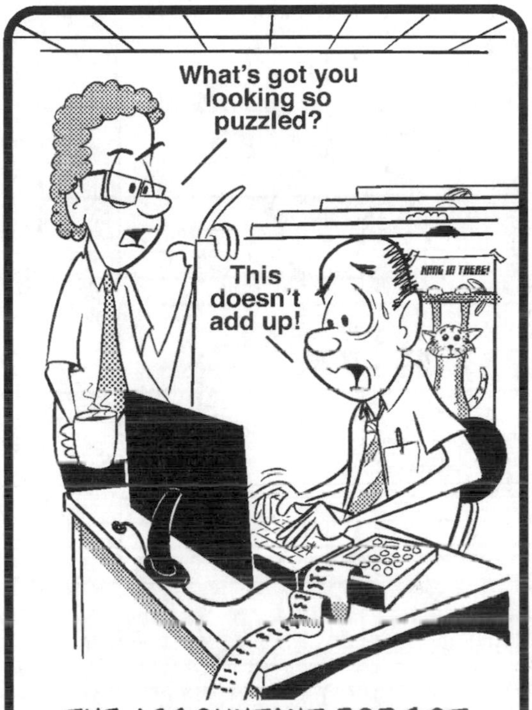

What's got you looking so puzzled?
This doesn't add up!

THE ACCOUNTANT FORGOT TO ADD THE LAST NUMBER ON THE PAGE AND SAT THERE ---

Now arrange the circled letters to form the surprise answer, as suggested by the above cartoon.

Print answer here

JUMBLE®

Unscramble these four Jumbles, one letter to each square, to form four ordinary words.

THYLO

ATNKE

TREATO

RWANDI

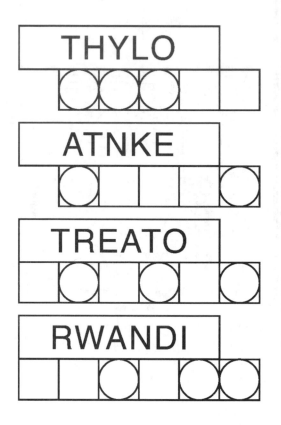

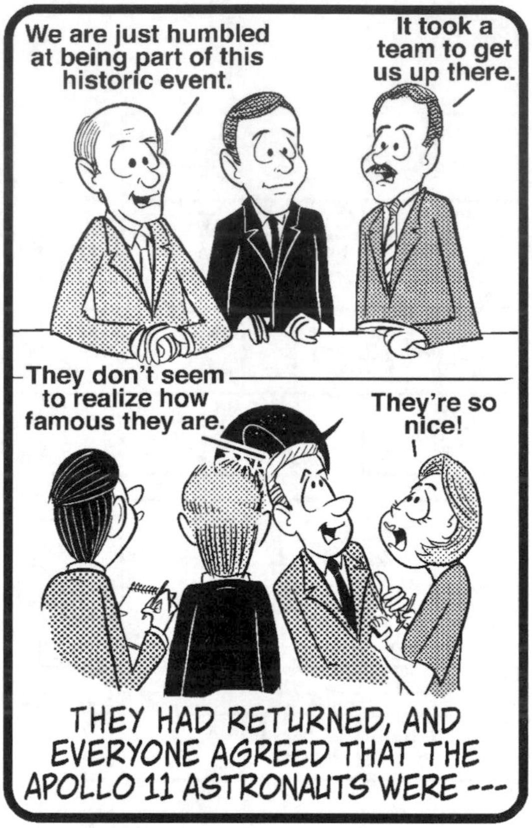
We are just humbled at being part of this historic event.
It took a team to get us up there.
They don't seem to realize how famous they are.
They're so nice!
THEY HAD RETURNED, AND EVERYONE AGREED THAT THE APOLLO 11 ASTRONAUTS WERE ---

Now arrange the circled letters to form the surprise answer, as suggested by the above cartoon.

Print answer here

PUZZLE

115

JUMBLE®

Unscramble these four Jumbles, one letter to each square, to form four ordinary words.

FSULH

WORFN

TOMONI

CILATI

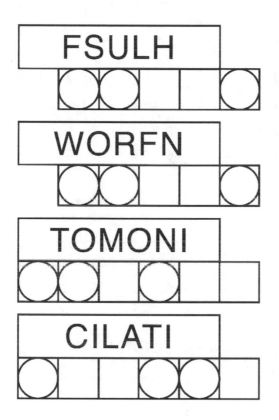

Tom called. He's not coming to fix the holes and cracks.
He texted me earlier. I'll take care of his work.
THE CAULK AND PUTTY GUY WAS OUT, BUT THERE WAS SOMEONE ELSE WHO COULD ---

Now arrange the circled letters to form the surprise answer, as suggested by the above cartoon.

Print answer here

PUZZLE

116

Unscramble these four Jumbles, one letter to each square, to form four ordinary words.

SAYET

RIFTL

CNAPUK

LVTEEV

I'm really struggling when I throw the ball into the air.
We'll have you acing people in no time.
THE PLAYER WORKED WITH THE TENNIS INSTRUCTOR IN AN ATTEMPT TO FIX HER ---

Now arrange the circled letters to form the surprise answer, as suggested by the above cartoon.

Print answer here

PUZZLE

117

JUMBLE®

Unscramble these four Jumbles, one letter to each square, to form four ordinary words.

LIVAL

GLTIH

GENUHO

PMCASU

We'll have a great view of our little bay!
It's coming along.

THEY WANTED A BETTER VIEW OF THE SMALL INLET FROM THEIR HOME, SO THEY BUILT AN ---

Now arrange the circled letters to form the surprise answer, as suggested by the above cartoon.

Print answer here

PUZZLE

118

JUMBLE®

Unscramble these four Jumbles, one letter to each square, to form four ordinary words.

THWCA

SYHTA

SIMACO

CTALEK

Wow! Are you going to sell these?
I'm going to fly from place to place making sales.
THE OSPREY ARTIST CREATED ORIGINAL PAINTINGS AND PLANNED TO ---

Now arrange the circled letters to form the surprise answer, as suggested by the above cartoon.

Print answer here

PUZZLE

119

JUMBLE®

Unscramble these four Jumbles, one letter to each square, to form four ordinary words.

DOVIE

LORDL

DMULED

TUAARM

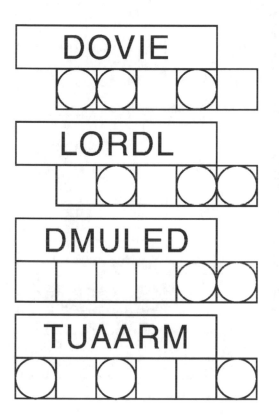

It was always tough to get my five brothers and sisters together for pictures.
Her family reunions are huge.
I bet my wife's are bigger.
That's nothing! I come from a family of nine.
SHE THOUGHT SHE CAME FROM A LARGE FAMILY, BUT IT'S ---

Now arrange the circled letters to form the surprise answer, as suggested by the above cartoon.

Print answer here

PUZZLE

120

JUMBLE®

Unscramble these four Jumbles, one letter to each square, to form four ordinary words.

RUBLT

TIYKT

FLANIE

DHENDI

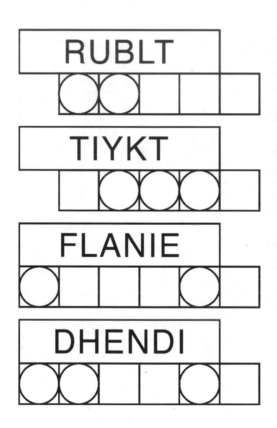

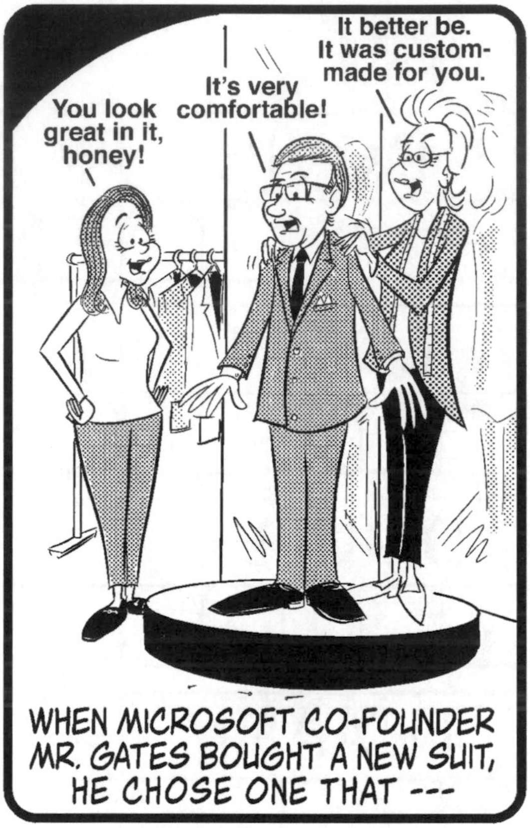

You look great in it, honey!
It's very comfortable!
It better be. It was custom-made for you.

WHEN MICROSOFT CO-FOUNDER MR. GATES BOUGHT A NEW SUIT, HE CHOSE ONE THAT ---

Now arrange the circled letters to form the surprise answer, as suggested by the above cartoon.

Print answer here

PUZZLE

121

JUMBLE®

Unscramble these four Jumbles, one letter to each square, to form four ordinary words.

RACYR

SUDEO

TUNIOG

NOLLEY

Let's go, people! My train is leaving in 10 seconds.
THE SUBWAY TRAIN OPERATOR WAS IN CHARGE AND HAD EVERYTHING ---

Now arrange the circled letters to form the surprise answer, as suggested by the above cartoon.

Print answer here

PUZZLE

122

JUMBLE®

Unscramble these four Jumbles, one letter to each square, to form four ordinary words.

DXUEE

SOLSF

TOOLNI

DNACEN

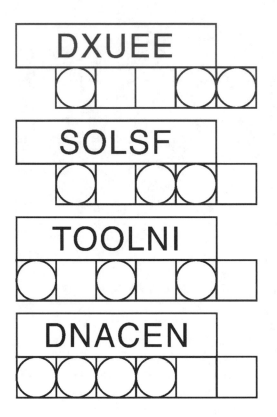

Maybe if you weren't in such a hurry, you would have seen this isn't the exit.
Wow! That was fast!

WHEN HE RAN OVER THE TIRE SPIKES, HIS FRONT TIRES LOST AIR IN ---

Now arrange the circled letters to form the surprise answer, as suggested by the above cartoon.

Print answer here

PUZZLE

123

JUMBLE®

Unscramble these four Jumbles, one letter to each square, to form four ordinary words.

ALGED

NGROP

SCAWEH

FLYUEE

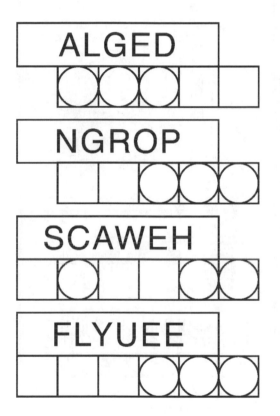

They're so loud!
This is obscene!
THE BEACHGOERS DIDN'T APPRECIATE THE SEAGULLS' OBNOXIOUSLY LOUD AND ---

Now arrange the circled letters to form the surprise answer, as suggested by the above cartoon.

Print answer here " "

PUZZLE

124

JUMBLE®

Unscramble these four Jumbles, one letter to each square, to form four ordinary words.

LIYMK

OCNUE

BPRAUT

SYRAGS

First off, tell me how you got in this condition.
How much time do you have?
HE WAS HAVING PAIN IN HIS LUMBAR REGION, AND THE CHIROPRACTOR WANTED THE ---

Now arrange the circled letters to form the surprise answer, as suggested by the above cartoon.

Print answer here

PUZZLE

125

JUMBLE®

Unscramble these four Jumbles, one letter to each square, to form four ordinary words.

BEALF

FROEF

CUVAMU

SKURNH

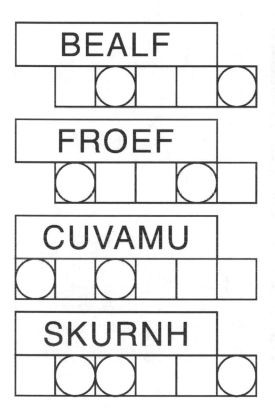

JUMBLETOWN LANDFILL
This is chaos! There's no more room.
That smell is awful!

THE TOWN'S LANDFILL WAS OVER CAPACITY AND BEGINNING TO ---

Now arrange the circled letters to form the surprise answer, as suggested by the above cartoon.

Print answer here " "

PUZZLE

126

JUMBLE®

Unscramble these four Jumbles, one letter to each square, to form four ordinary words.

SERTC

CKNKA

NOREDY

TORESE

With our successful launches, we are expanding our business.
AFTER SO MANY SUCCESSFUL LAUNCHES, SPACEX REVENUE WAS BEGINNING TO ---

Now arrange the circled letters to form the surprise answer, as suggested by the above cartoon.

Print answer here

PUZZLE

127

JUMBLE®

Unscramble these four Jumbles, one letter to each square, to form four ordinary words.

LRIGL

NRUKT

DYBOON

GRHITB

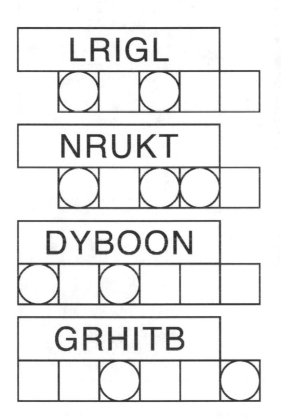

Look out! Here I come!
Do you mind?
No one asked you!
THE INTERRUPTING RAM WAS BEING RUDE. THEY DIDN'T APPRECIATE HIM ---

Now arrange the circled letters to form the surprise answer, as suggested by the above cartoon.

Print answer here

PUZZLE

128

JUMBLE®

Unscramble these four Jumbles, one letter to each square, to form four ordinary words.

CLUKY

RDONU

LOTIVE

VIRHET

JUMBLE DOWNS
WIN PLACE SHOW
He left the gate ready to win!
No one came close!
WHEN THE RACEHORSE GOT OFF TO SUCH A GREAT START RIGHT OUT OF THE GATE, IT ---

Now arrange the circled letters to form the surprise answer, as suggested by the above cartoon.

Print answer here

PUZZLE

129

JUMBLE®

Unscramble these four Jumbles, one letter to each square, to form four ordinary words.

TWYIT

BOREX

NNEEIG

SENSAO

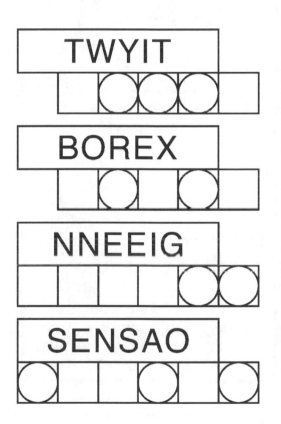

Would you knock $50 off?
The price is the price. You can't find marble bookends like these anywhere.
Just pay the price.
THE PRICE OF THE ANTIQUE MARBLE BOOKENDS WAS ---

Now arrange the circled letters to form the surprise answer, as suggested by the above cartoon.

Print answer here

PUZZLE

130

JUMBLE®

Unscramble these four Jumbles, one letter to each square, to form four ordinary words.

NUPDO

GBSOU

NIRDAC

LENGUJ

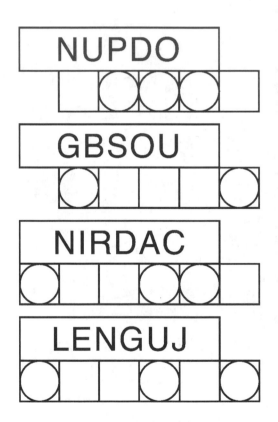

I assume you can start right away?
I sure can!

HE WOULD BE HAPPY TO START WORK AS THEIR NEW NIGHT WATCHMAN AFTER ---

Now arrange the circled letters to form the surprise answer, as suggested by the above cartoon.

Print answer here ⬜⬜⬜⬜⬜⬜⬜⬜ **THE** ⬜⬜⬜

PUZZLE

131

JUMBLE®

Unscramble these four Jumbles, one letter to each square, to form four ordinary words.

OTRIA

UDEFG

CESKTO

CANLYU

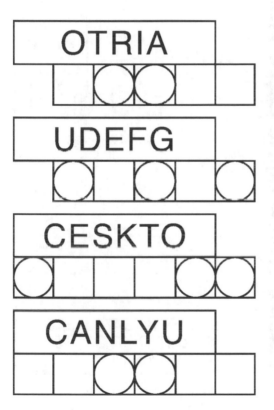

It securely holds the garment together.
Do it again!
I can't stop watching it!
It's ingenious!
WHEN GIDEON SUNDBACK SHOWED HOW HIS NEW ZIPPER WORKED, PEOPLE WERE ---

Now arrange the circled letters to form the surprise answer, as suggested by the above cartoon.

Print answer here " - "

PUZZLE

132

JUMBLE®

Unscramble these four Jumbles, one letter to each square, to form four ordinary words.

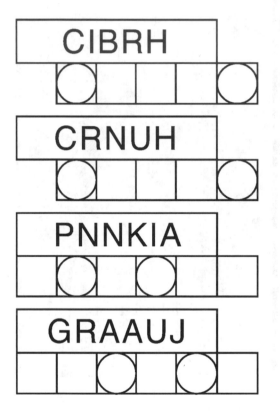

CIBRH

CRNUH

PNNKIA

GRAAUJ

I'm not feeling it today.
It will be nice to have the cave to ourselves for once.
MOST OF THE BATS WERE FLYING OUT OF THE CAVE, BUT A FEW DECIDED TO ---

Now arrange the circled letters to form the surprise answer, as suggested by the above cartoon.

Print answer here

PUZZLE

133

JUMBLE®

Unscramble these four Jumbles, one letter to each square, to form four ordinary words.

TAMLE

SAAIL

RHITTS

UJRINO

You're lucky you two are so cute!
It was his idea.
We just wanted to dress up like a hero. Like you, Mommy.
EVEN WHEN THE TWINS MISBEHAVED, SHE LOVED THEM ---

Now arrange the circled letters to form the surprise answer, as suggested by the above cartoon.

Print answer here THE

PUZZLE

134

JUMBLE®

Unscramble these four Jumbles, one letter to each square, to form four ordinary words.

RETWH

ALGEE

LAHNIE

VINDIE

Arm Wrestling Championship
This is going to be gripping! Who will be champ?
TO SEE WHO WAS THE BEST ARM WRESTLER, THEY ---

Now arrange the circled letters to form the surprise answer, as suggested by the above cartoon.

Print answer here

PUZZLE

135

JUMBLE®

Unscramble these four Jumbles, one letter to each square, to form four ordinary words.

RMEAF

KRAFN

TFUIOT

GEEEMR

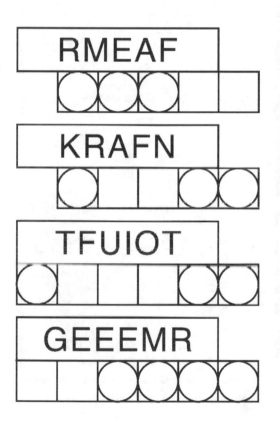

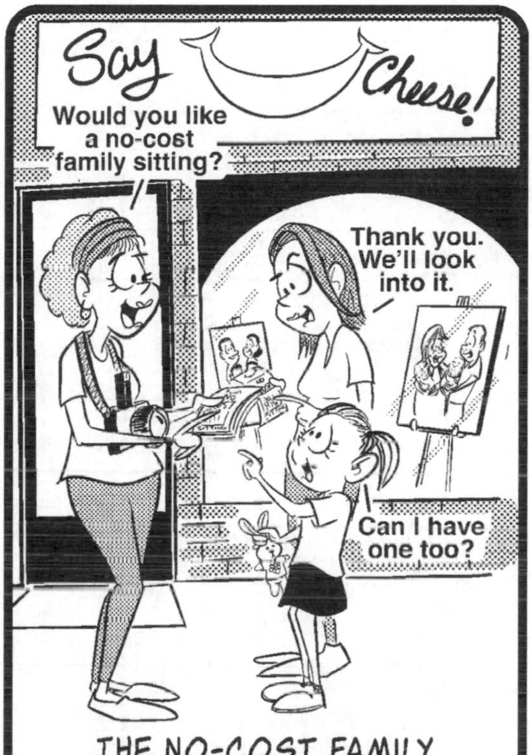
Say Cheese!
Would you like a no-cost family sitting?
Thank you. We'll look into it.
Can I have one too?
THE NO-COST FAMILY PHOTO COUPONS WERE ---

Now arrange the circled letters to form the surprise answer, as suggested by the above cartoon.

Print answer here ____ ___ THE _______

PUZZLE

136

JUMBLE®

Unscramble these four Jumbles, one letter to each square, to form four ordinary words.

SOKKI

NYRNU

YLEMEK

CCSUTA

I can't wait to start digging. I know there is gold in those hills!
Is that all you talk about?
DURING THE CALIFORNIA GOLD RUSH, THIS LAND OWNER HAD A ---

Now arrange the circled letters to form the surprise answer, as suggested by the above cartoon.

Print answer here ___ - _____ " ____ "

PUZZLE

137

JUMBLE®

Unscramble these four Jumbles, one letter to each square, to form four ordinary words.

LIGAE

RADHO

RRTEEF

CDTEKO

Now arrange the circled letters to form the surprise answer, as suggested by the above cartoon.

Print answer here

PUZZLE

138

JUMBLE®

Unscramble these four Jumbles, one letter to each square, to form four ordinary words.

RUBYL

PAATD

SJYULT

MOONDI

Why would you go to a cemetery at night?
They do in all these horror movies.
BEN BETTER
THE HORROR MOVIE SET IN THE CEMETERY HAD A ---

Now arrange the circled letters to form the surprise answer, as suggested by the above cartoon.

Print answer here

PUZZLE

139

JUMBLE®

Unscramble these four Jumbles, one letter to each square, to form four ordinary words.

TIDOT

NEETV

GHUBOT

TMEENC

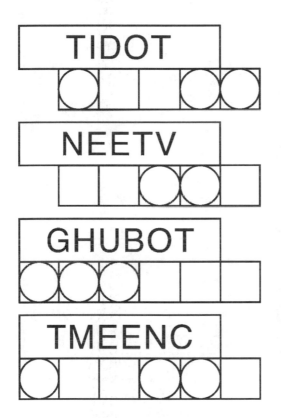

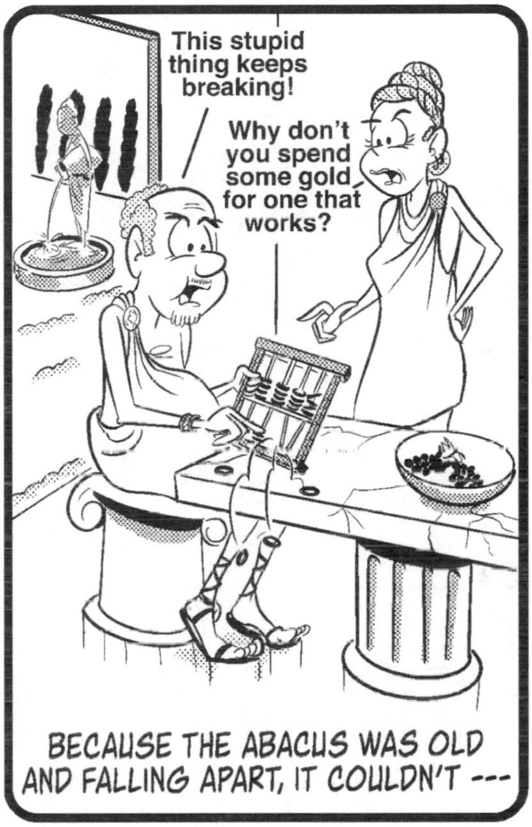

This stupid thing keeps breaking!
Why don't you spend some gold for one that works?
BECAUSE THE ABACUS WAS OLD AND FALLING APART, IT COULDN'T ---

Now arrange the circled letters to form the surprise answer, as suggested by the above cartoon.

Print answer here

PUZZLE

140

JUMBLE®

Unscramble these four Jumbles, one letter to each square, to form four ordinary words.

SYLYH

ODMME

RRHOBA

FIYNAM

You guys have this down.
We run a tight ship.
D-F
G-J
Is this where I pick up my outfit?
Yes! May I have your name? Then I'll show you where to go.
THEY DISTRIBUTED THE HOSPITAL ATTENDANTS' NEW UNIFORMS IN AN ---

Now arrange the circled letters to form the surprise answer, as suggested by the above cartoon.

Print answer here

PUZZLE

141

JUMBLE®

Unscramble these four Jumbles, one letter to each square, to form four ordinary words.

NOOHR

TECIH

LNEETG

LMAYCL

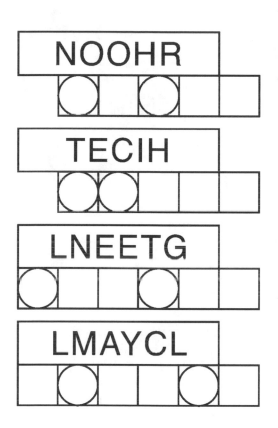

I've had enough. I'm going to bed.
Have you not heard anything I've said?
The python is not longer.
THEY DISCUSSED RETICULATED PYTHONS AND ANACONDAS ---

Now arrange the circled letters to form the surprise answer, as suggested by the above cartoon.

Print answer here

PUZZLE

142

JUMBLE®

Unscramble these four Jumbles, one letter to each square, to form four ordinary words.

ORÉPA

KKANC

NHRCCU

TULEDI

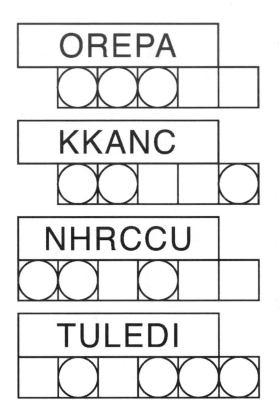

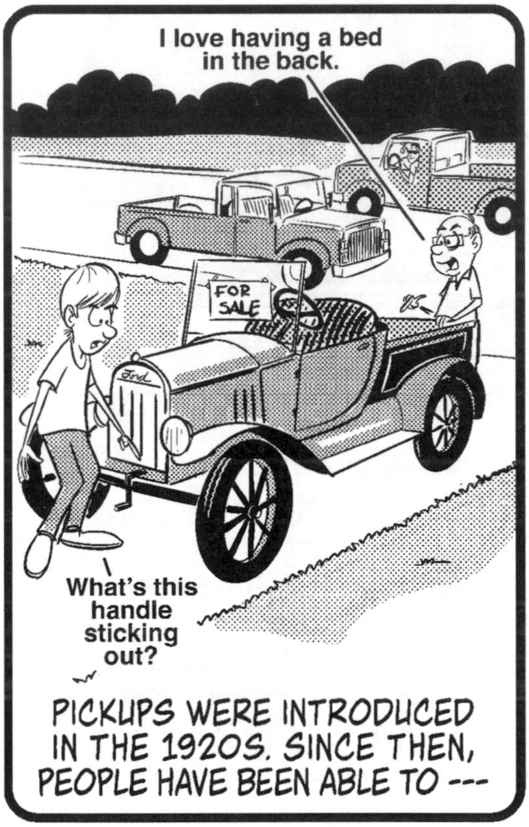
I love having a bed in the back.
FOR SALE
What's this handle sticking out?
PICKUPS WERE INTRODUCED IN THE 1920S. SINCE THEN, PEOPLE HAVE BEEN ABLE TO ---

Now arrange the circled letters to form the surprise answer, as suggested by the above cartoon.

Print answer here

PUZZLE

143

JUMBLE®

Unscramble these four Jumbles, one letter to each square, to form four ordinary words.

HUCOC

GNIES

RAAYIV

TUWALO

You tied them again!
Once you learn to pull the bunny ears back, tightening them is easy!
AFTER SHE LEARNED TO CONSISTENTLY TIE HER OWN SHOES, ---

Now arrange the circled letters to form the surprise answer, as suggested by the above cartoon.

Print answer here

PUZZLE

144

JUMBLE®

Unscramble these four Jumbles, one letter to each square, to form four ordinary words.

TOCHL

KALYE

DESEYP

NUGLEO

What kind of filth is that?
I'm not sure this is good for the kids.
Look at him move!
Look! I'm Elvis!!

ELVIS PRESLEY'S 1957 HIT SONG HAD SOME PEOPLE ---

Now arrange the circled letters to form the surprise answer, as suggested by the above cartoon.

Print answer here

PUZZLE

145

JUMBLE®

Unscramble these four Jumbles, one letter to each square, to form four ordinary words.

RSEDS

SNUWG

LWDIME

THYACC

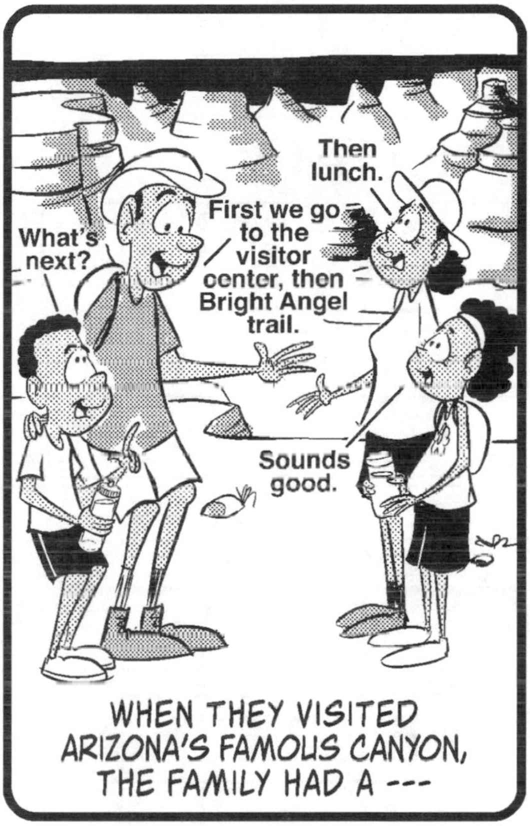
What's next?
First we go to the visitor center, then Bright Angel trail.
Then lunch.
Sounds good.
WHEN THEY VISITED ARIZONA'S FAMOUS CANYON, THE FAMILY HAD A ---

Now arrange the circled letters to form the surprise answer, as suggested by the above cartoon.

Print answer here

PUZZLE

146

JUMBLE®

Unscramble these four Jumbles, one letter to each square, to form four ordinary words.

CCAOO

FINEK

TILLET

FDESEU

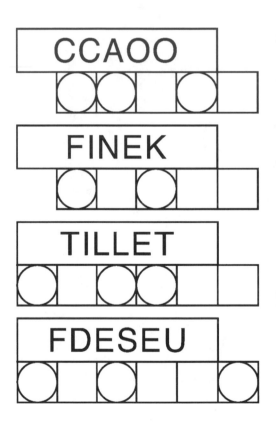

Looks like everyone's excited about this movie.
ALFRED HITCHCOCK PRESENTS
THE BIRDS

WHEN ALFRED HITCHCOCK'S MOVIE, "THE BIRDS," PREMIERED IN 1963, PEOPLE ---

Now arrange the circled letters to form the surprise answer, as suggested by the above cartoon.

Print answer here

PUZZLE

147

JUMBLE®

Unscramble these four Jumbles, one letter to each square, to form four ordinary words.

CNIEM

SLEYT

PRILSA

PONCAY

Well done, sir.
This is a great way to honor those who served.

MAKING NOV. 11 AN OFFICIAL HOLIDAY TO HONOR VETERANS WAS A GREAT IDEA ---

Now arrange the circled letters to form the surprise answer, as suggested by the above cartoon.

Print answer here

PUZZLE

148

JUMBLE®

Unscramble these four Jumbles, one letter to each square, to form four ordinary words.

GEMAO

WTAHE

NINOMI

CTILHG

You need to not worry so much. It doesn't help.
I can't stop thinking about dieting.
THE LACK OF SUCCESS WITH HIS DIET WAS ---

Now arrange the circled letters to form the surprise answer, as suggested by the above cartoon.

Print answer here

PUZZLE

149

JUMBLE®

Unscramble these four Jumbles, one letter to each square, to form four ordinary words.

TIDEY

NTALS

NAYRAC

VIRQUE

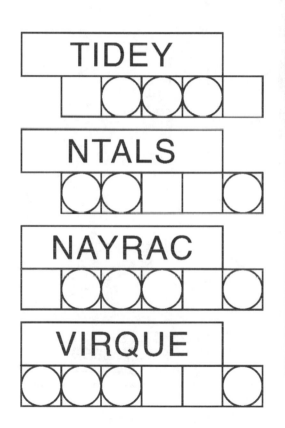

We landed — right where we planned.
It's so calm and peaceful here.
AFTER APOLLO 11 TOUCHED DOWN ON THE MOON, THE ASTRONAUTS COULD ---

Now arrange the circled letters to form the surprise answer, as suggested by the above cartoon.

Print answer here “ ”

PUZZLE

150

JUMBLE®

Unscramble these four Jumbles, one letter to each square, to form four ordinary words.

TOAQU

SULHF

GSATIM

MEGINL

Is this professional grade?
You have an excellent eye! That's our finest hammer.

THE CARPENTER SHOPPED FOR A NEW HAMMER THAT WOULD BE ---

Now arrange the circled letters to form the surprise answer, as suggested by the above cartoon.

Print answer here

JUMBLE®

Unscramble these four Jumbles, one letter to each square, to form four ordinary words.

SULYO

RLIDL

TUABEY

LDEPEG

Today's Guest JUMBLER is
RUSSELL MYERS
Creator of BROOM-HILDA

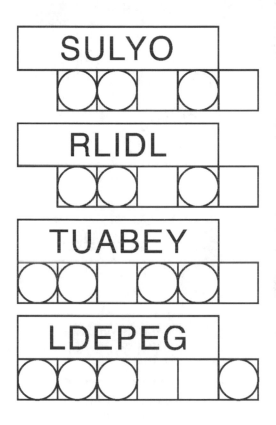

ANOTHER MISFIRE?
NOBODY'S PERFECT!
MY TURN TO FETCH THE FIRE HOSE!
RUSSELL MYERS

WHEN BROOM-HILDA'S MAGIC BACKFIRED, IT ---

Now arrange the circled letters to form the surprise answer, as suggested by the above cartoon.

Print answer here

PUZZLE

152

JUMBLE®

Unscramble these four Jumbles, one letter to each square, to form four ordinary words.

RAYWE

RFDAT

MPAISH

LYOGMO

Today's Guest JUMBLER is
JAN ELIOT
Creator of STONE SOUP

SEE YA LATER, VALERIE.
VAL WAS SILENT WHEN HOLLY CALLED HER BY HER FIRST NAME, EVEN THOUGH—

Now arrange the circled letters to form the surprise answer, as suggested by the above cartoon.

Print answer here " ' "

PUZZLE

153

JUMBLE®

Unscramble these four Jumbles, one letter to each square, to form four ordinary words.

NUSTT

NABDR

LIGGGE

BTORHE

I've won six world championships.
Have you beaten Ralph Macchio?
WHEN IT COMES TO KARATE, CHUCK NORRIS HAS NUMEROUS ACCOMPLISHMENTS ---

Now arrange the circled letters to form the surprise answer, as suggested by the above cartoon.

Print answer here

PUZZLE

154

JUMBLE®

Unscramble these four Jumbles, one letter to each square, to form four ordinary words.

GREVE

THACC

ESSUTN

DNORIO

Now that I've been able to see the model and the drawings, I understand what you're envisioning.
I'm glad we had this conversation. We should be good to go.
THE CONVERSATION BETWEEN THE ARCHITECT AND GENERAL CONTRACTOR WAS ---

Now arrange the circled letters to form the surprise answer, as suggested by the above cartoon.

Print answer here

JUMBLE®

Unscramble these four Jumbles, one letter to each square, to form four ordinary words.

BROOT

LIEDY

PNRSIG

KWAANE

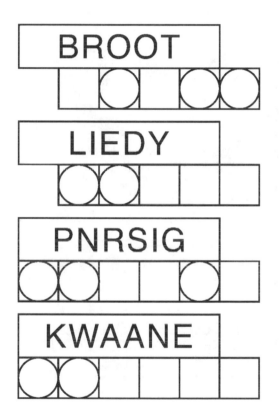

I think this route is the fastest.
What do you think about the scenic route instead?
MAP WORLD
BEFORE THEY CHOSE A ROUTE TO TRAVEL, THEY LOOKED AT THE MAP TO ---

Now arrange the circled letters to form the surprise answer, as suggested by the above cartoon.

Print answer here " ◯◯◯ " THEIR ◯◯◯◯◯◯◯

PUZZLE 156

JUMBLE®

Unscramble these four Jumbles, one letter to each square, to form four ordinary words.

TELFE

NLUPK

LEWBOL

WAREYL

Time for my annual post-turkey-gobbling nap.
We were counting on it.
How do you eat so much every year?

WHEN IT COMES TO THANKSGIVING TURKEY, HE TENDED TO EAT A LOT, WHICH HE ---

Now arrange the circled letters to form the surprise answer, as suggested by the above cartoon.

Print answer here

PUZZLE

157

JUMBLE®

Unscramble these four Jumbles, one letter to each square, to form four ordinary words.

MEEEC

COTTE

LCASLU

NROOBC

Keep trying! Don't let it bother you. You'll get it.
Wow! That's interesting. Good job!
THE YOUNG MUSICIAN COULDN'T GET THE HIGH NOTES JUST RIGHT AND FOUND THEM ---

Now arrange the circled letters to form the surprise answer, as suggested by the above cartoon.

Print answer here "______ - ____"

PUZZLE

158

JUMBLE®

Unscramble these four Jumbles, one letter to each square, to form four ordinary words.

LUFAT

FYOLT

SSLUYT

UMIENM

Have you tried this? It's so good!
This place is so elegant.
THEY THOROUGHLY ENJOYED THE FLAVORS OF THEIR FOOD IN A RESTAURANT THAT WAS DECORATED ---

Now arrange the circled letters to form the surprise answer, as suggested by the above cartoon.

Print answer here

PUZZLE 159

JUMBLE®

Unscramble these four Jumbles, one letter to each square, to form four ordinary words.

LUYRT

SELSB

WPARSL

BERROD

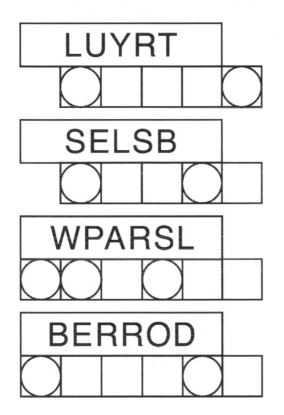

She's finally doing it!
Little by little, she caught on!

THE PROCESS OF AN INFANT BECOMING A TODDLER INVOLVES ---

Now arrange the circled letters to form the surprise answer, as suggested by the above cartoon.

Print answer here

PUZZLE

160

JUMBLE®

Unscramble these four Jumbles, one letter to each square, to form four ordinary words.

ELABK

GDDEO

SOYLGS

CTTHAA

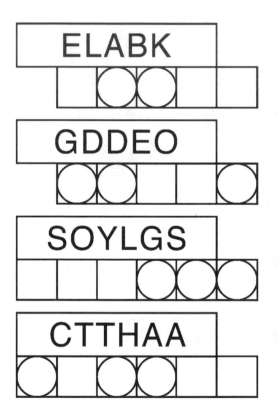

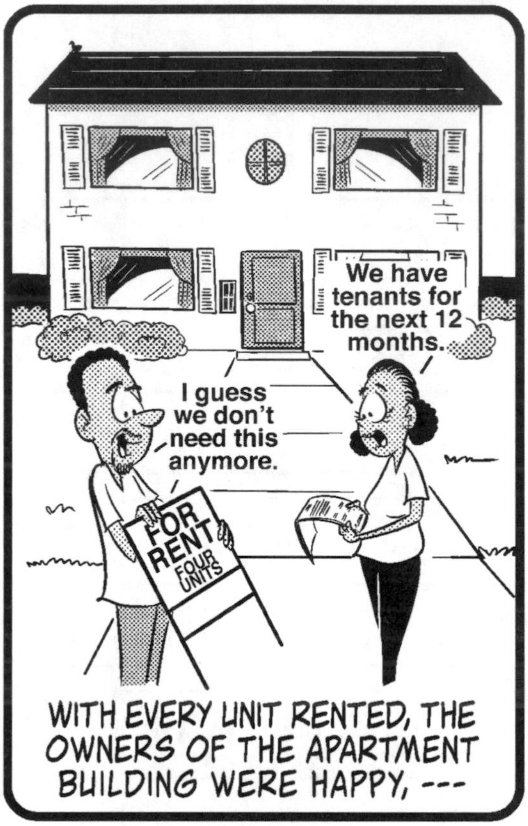
We have tenants for the next 12 months.
I guess we don't need this anymore.
FOR RENT FOUR UNITS
WITH EVERY UNIT RENTED, THE OWNERS OF THE APARTMENT BUILDING WERE HAPPY, ---

Now arrange the circled letters to form the surprise answer, as suggested by the above cartoon.

Print answer here ◯◯ ◯◯◯ THE "◯◯◯◯◯◯"

JUMBLE®

HEiST

CHALLENGER PUZZLES

PUZZLE

161

JUMBLE®

Unscramble these six Jumbles, one letter to each square, to form six ordinary words.

GREBID

YETLEE

RANCAL

VERABE

SAUCCU

PITTEO

THE MISER'S FAVORITE SALAD.

Now arrange the circled letters to form the surprise answer, as suggested by the above cartoon.

Print answer here

&

JUMBLE®

Unscramble these six Jumbles, one letter to each square, to form six ordinary words.

YIMWAD

VIKONE

HARSHT

YENLOP

ENERGE

KANTIE

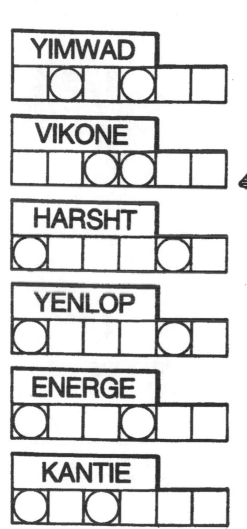

WHAT THE BARTENDER SAID THAT CAUSED THE MARTINI DRINKER TO THINK OF DICKENS.

Now arrange the circled letters to form the surprise answer, as suggested by the above cartoon.

Print answer here

"◯◯◯◯◯ ◯◯ ◯◯◯◯◯◯?"

PUZZLE

163

JUMBLE®

Unscramble these six Jumbles, one letter to each square, to form six ordinary words.

LENETS

TACHUG

CAPUTE

FELGUN

YORCUT

LAWVOA

That's my Pop!
POSSIBLY HIS MALE OFFSPRING AT THE RECITAL.

Now arrange the circled letters to form the surprise answer, as suggested by the above cartoon.

Print answer here

" - - "

JUMBLE®

Unscramble these six Jumbles, one letter to each square, to form six ordinary words.

BRUHEC

PLUBAR

RAHGEC

INBOUN

VOCENX

INTOUG

WHAT THE PSYCHIATRIST'S CRABBY PATIENT WAS.

Now arrange the circled letters to form the surprise answer, as suggested by the above cartoon.

Print answer here

A ◯◯◯◯◯◯ ◯◯ A ◯◯◯◯◯

PUZZLE

165

JUMBLE®

Unscramble these six Jumbles, one letter to each square, to form six ordinary words.

TUPPIL

LIRMAN

STEACK

HYNWIN

THARGE

TAPHAY

HE MAKES A NICE LIVING WITHOUT DOING A DAY'S WORK.

Now arrange the circled letters to form the surprise answer, as suggested by the above cartoon.

Print answer here

A

PUZZLE

166

JUMBLE®

Unscramble these six Jumbles, one letter to each square, to form six ordinary words.

SAVILE

ODONEL

TIVNAY

YESWIL

RUBENK

TANDLE

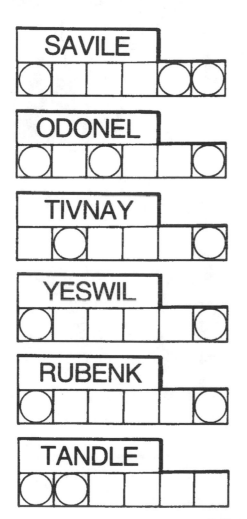

DO YOU SERVE CRABS HERE?

Now arrange the circled letters to form the surprise answer, as suggested by the above cartoon.

Print answer here

" ◯◯ ◯◯◯◯◯◯ ◯◯◯◯◯◯◯ "

PUZZLE 167

JUMBLE®

Unscramble these six Jumbles, one letter to each square, to form six ordinary words.

CEPTID

ZALBER

RELPHE

RISDAM

GOULEY

TENGLE

Delicious
THIS FOOD ITEM CAN'T BE BEAT!

Now arrange the circled letters to form the surprise answer, as suggested by the above cartoon.

Print answer here

A ◯◯◯◯ - ◯◯◯◯◯◯ ◯◯◯

PUZZLE

168

JUMBLE®

Unscramble these six Jumbles, one letter to each square, to form six ordinary words.

STAARY

GREATY

CORRET

YIKELL

ZAMONA

LIDIAN

I hope I have enough collateral
BANK
SALOON
DRY GOODS.
WHO WAS THAT FAMOUS INDIAN LOOKING FOR IN THE BANK?

Now arrange the circled letters to form the surprise answer, as suggested by the above cartoon.

Print answer here

THE " "

PUZZLE

169

JUMBLE®

Unscramble these six Jumbles, one letter to each square, to form six ordinary words.

GATNIC

VYCOON

SOXEEP

CRIMET

MINTEY

INCOVE

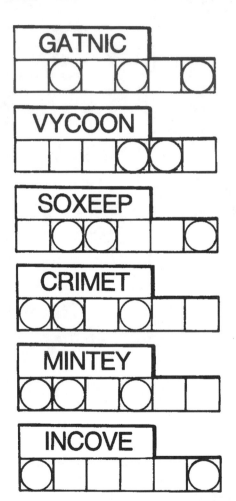

After all these years, we'll (sob) miss you

LEAVING THE NEIGHBORHOOD PROVED TO BE THIS.

Now arrange the circled letters to form the surprise answer, as suggested by the above cartoon.

Print answer here

A " "

PUZZLE

170

JUMBLE®

Unscramble these six Jumbles, one letter to each square, to form six ordinary words.

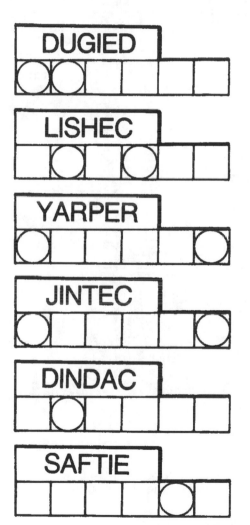

HOW DID THE ASTRONAUT LIKE HIS EGGS?

DUGIED

LISHEC

YARPER

JINTEC

DINDAC

SAFTIE

Now arrange the circled letters to form the surprise answer, as suggested by the above cartoon.

Print answer here

PUZZLE

171

JUMBLE®

Unscramble these six Jumbles, one letter to each square, to form six ordinary words.

ZRAHDA

VINTAE

PRUYYS

EEBARK

LIPTER

LWEFOL

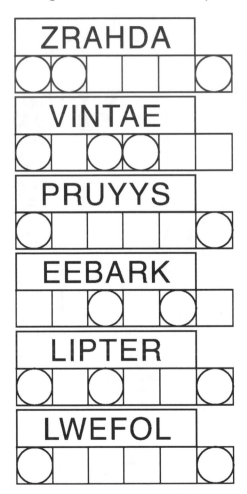

I don't know what happened.
We'll figure out why he passed out, Ma'am.
We'll check you out, Sir.
The last thing I remember is looking for the pretzel place.

HE'D PASSED OUT WHILE SHOPPING, AND THEY DIDN'T HAVE THE ---

Now arrange the circled letters to form the surprise answer, as suggested by the above cartoon.

Print answer here

PUZZLE

172

JUMBLE®

Unscramble these six Jumbles, one letter to each square, to form six ordinary words.

LAGIOE

WAQKUS

MARFTO

NNNCAO

CABEHL

MEFLEA

I can't believe it! I'm so excited. I can't wait to celebrate.
Nice shot! Congratulations!
SHE'D JUST WON THE RACQUETBALL TOURNAMENT AND WAS ---

Now arrange the circled letters to form the surprise answer, as suggested by the above cartoon.

Print answer here

________ ___ THE ______

PUZZLE

173

JUMBLE®

Unscramble these six Jumbles, one letter to each square, to form six ordinary words.

AMDWEO

BZAOEG

TINBET

RENPOS

CUGORH

FHIRTT

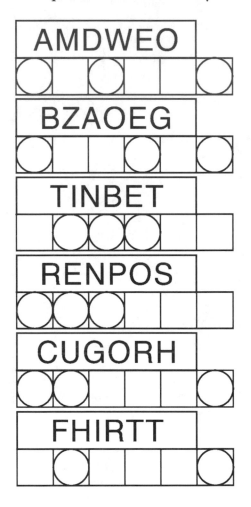

How do you explain the success of your operating system?
They seem to like the ease of operation.
MICROSOFT
Is it all on just three floppies?

AFTER MICROSOFT LAUNCHED WINDOWS, IT DIDN'T TAKE LONG FOR PEOPLE TO ---

Now arrange the circled letters to form the surprise answer, as suggested by the above cartoon.

Print answer here

PUZZLE

174

JUMBLE®

Unscramble these six Jumbles, one letter to each square, to form six ordinary words.

NGRADO

MYESST

SLAUWR

LYOGOM

ESOLON

SOFLIS

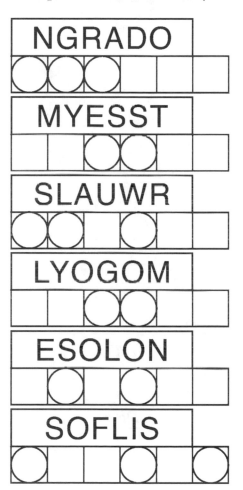

What am I supposed to make with J,W,K,V,P,L,H?
I've just gotten lucky with my letters today.

THE SCRABBLE PLAYER WAS DOWN BY MORE THAN 200 POINTS AND ---

Now arrange the circled letters to form the surprise answer, as suggested by the above cartoon.

Print answer here

PUZZLE

175

JUMBLE®

Unscramble these six Jumbles, one letter to each square, to form six ordinary words.

TTMOOA

TRAGEY

DANCID

TDEESL

HYIGLH

GEEDUL

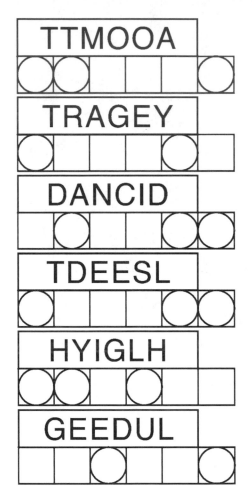

There's nobody scarier than you. You're amazing!
Stop it. I just do the best I can with what I have.
Don't be modest. People are scared to death of you.
EVERYONE KNEW SLEEPY HOLLOW'S INFAMOUS HORSEMAN, BUT HE DIDN'T ---

Now arrange the circled letters to form the surprise answer, as suggested by the above cartoon.

Print answer here

PUZZLE

176

JUMBLE®

Unscramble these six Jumbles, one letter to each square, to form six ordinary words.

RWANDO

CAPERN

TROHET

WRUOFR

VEYTIL

TWOALU

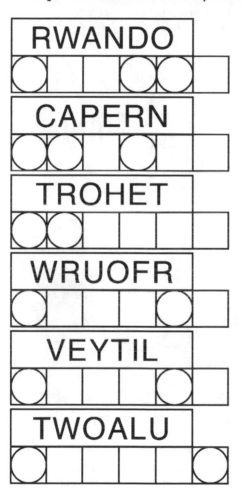

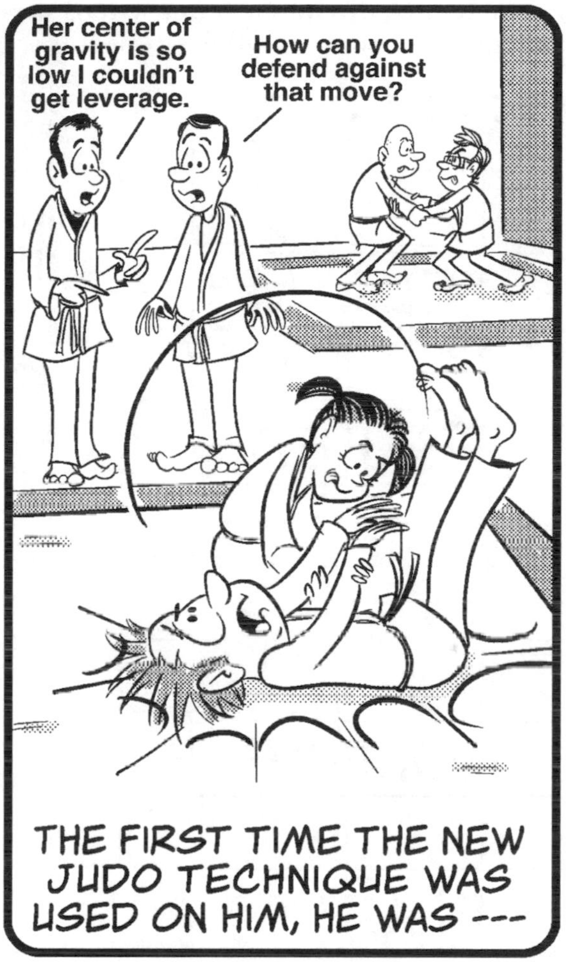
Her center of gravity is so low I couldn't get leverage.
How can you defend against that move?
THE FIRST TIME THE NEW JUDO TECHNIQUE WAS USED ON HIM, HE WAS ---

Now arrange the circled letters to form the surprise answer, as suggested by the above cartoon.

Print answer here

PUZZLE

177

JUMBLE®

Unscramble these six Jumbles, one letter to each square, to form six ordinary words.

VAYSRO

TELALM

TEAFED

TVENIS

ROMMIE

FNUPIF

John, Paul, George and Ringo are at it again with more number one songs than anyone else this year! Here's their latest, "I Feel Fine"!
AMER
B STAND

WHEN IT CAME TO #1 SONGS IN 1964, THE BEATLES WERE ---

Now arrange the circled letters to form the surprise answer, as suggested by the above cartoon.

Print answer here

PUZZLE

178

JUMBLE®

Unscramble these six Jumbles, one letter to each square, to form six ordinary words.

LANMOS

DDDAEP

HONKOU

RVLEEC

COLEAL

SULHBE

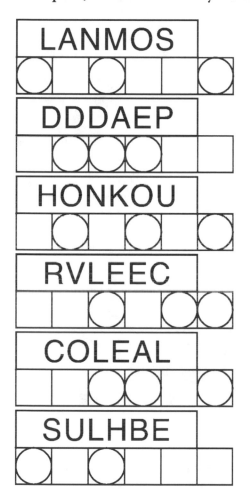

They ended in the nick of time!
We need to beat the rain!
We'd better run!
THEY ENDED THE CONCERT JUST BEFORE THE STORM HIT, AND THE AUDIENCE LEFT WITH ---

Now arrange the circled letters to form the surprise answer, as suggested by the above cartoon.

Print answer here

“ - - ”

PUZZLE

179

JUMBLE®

Unscramble these six Jumbles, one letter to each square, to form six ordinary words.

CAYNLU

DYARTW

TRAETM

LAPLOW

CLAPEA

DHULED

These are frozen rock-solid.
They will be ready for Thursday. Let's see what's next on the to-do list.
MR TURKEY
I YAM
DEFROSTING THE TURKEY DAYS BEFORE THANKSGIVING WAS A ---

Now arrange the circled letters to form the surprise answer, as suggested by the above cartoon.

Print answer here

“ ” -

PUZZLE
180

JUMBLE®

Unscramble these six Jumbles, one letter to each square, to form six ordinary words.

RMLOFA

GCCANO

RUYGEN

RSBPEU

TRUFHO

CADFEE

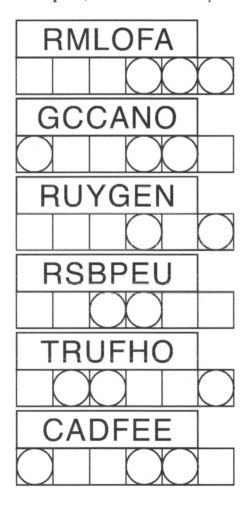

SPACEX
I've started this business so we can colonize Mars. I want this to be the farthest human life has ever traveled.

WHEN ELON MUSK FOUNDED SPACEX IN 2002, HE ---

Now arrange the circled letters to form the surprise answer, as suggested by the above cartoon.

Print answer here

Answers

1. **Jumbles:** SNARL LLAMA COUGAR ORIGIN
Answer: That egotistical cynic saw nothing good in the world, without the aid of this—A MIRROR

2. **Jumbles:** IDIOT FUZZY BROKER ATTAIN
Answer: What an astronaut has to be before he really starts working on the job—"FIRED"

3. **Jumbles:** EAGLE MEALY AFRAID DEBTOR
Answer: People go there to be this—"RE-FORMED"

4. **Jumbles:** POKER TEASE HYMNAL SURETY
Answer: What the game of polo involves a lot of—"HORSE PLAY"

5. **Jumbles:** TONIC ALBUM KNOTTY SLEIGH
Answer: Why they call them "tellers" at banks—MONEY ALWAYS "TALKS"

6. **Jumbles:** FELON LUCID WALRUS CLOTHE
Answer: What the young couple got when they went to the marriage counselor—A "WED-UCATION"

7. **Jumbles:** HOIST PARTY BUTTON DETACH
Answer: He aimed to please, but he was this—A BAD SHOT

8. **Jumbles:** SILKY HONOR CRAYON HUMBLE
Answer: If you want to succeed as a violinist, this is how you have to get involved with your music—UP TO YOUR CHIN

9. **Jumbles:** CIVIL BATHE TROUGH RELISH
Answer: Another name for writer's cramp—"AUTHORITIS" (arthritis)

10. **Jumbles:** ELITE ANNUL FLUNKY COMPEL
Answer: How he got the job—BY "KIN-FLUENCE"

11. **Jumbles:** BOWER PROBE TEAPOT FIDDLE
Answer: The hypochondriac changed doctors when he started to do this—FEEL BETTER

12. **Jumbles:** CRAFT ELDER BAZAAR FINERY
Answer: What he said when he couldn't find a decent pair of socks in his drawer—"DARN" IT!

13. **Jumbles:** JOINT FLOOR LOCKET VANDAL
Answer: What the coach kept saying to the team of zombies—LOOK ALIVE!

14. **Jumbles:** FUROR TABOO COWARD BASKET
Answer: Another name for the newly hatched termites—"BABES IN THE WOOD"

15. **Jumbles:** ELUDE HAVEN STUPID NATURE
Answer: The "tense" he used most frequently when making speeches—"PRE-TENSE"

16. **Jumbles:** PEACE DAILY CURFEW SMOKER
Answer: Could that smart cookie be this?—A WISE "CRACKER"

17. **Jumbles:** INEPT GUILT PIRATE FORBID
Answer: What people sometimes were during the Stone Age—"PETRIFIED"

18. **Jumbles:** SKULK LURID FAIRLY GENDER
Answer: What she called him when he went back on his promise to buy her a mink—A FINK

19. **Jumbles:** THYME IMPEL POCKET RADISH
Answer: Many a man is burned by picking up this—A HOT TIP

20. **Jumbles:** CHIDE AWOKE DONKEY WAITER
Answer: The conceited guy thinks if he had never been born, the world would do this—WONDER WHY

21. **Jumbles:** VAPOR JUMPY PAUPER YEARLY
Answer: The beginning of a dog's life might start when someone experiences this—PUPPY LOVE

22. **Jumbles:** TIGER RIVET DECODE PARLOR
Answer: For that gambler, this was the next thing to heaven—A "PAIR O' DICE" (paradise)

23. **Jumbles:** MOUND TWICE WAYLAY SPORTY
Answer: Although it won't necessarily make you rich, you might get this from an intelligent oyster—A PEARL OF WISDOM

24. **Jumbles:** EPOCH LYING BODILY OUTCRY
Answer: What the mountaineer's mascot was—"TOP DOG"

25. **Jumbles:** LYRIC MILKY UNLESS BUMPER
Answer: How to describe some of those late-night movies—"RERUN" OF THE MILL

26. **Jumbles:** OZONE NEWLY SUBURB KOWTOW
Answer: He had to give her a fake diamond because he was this—"STONE" BROKE

27. **Jumbles:** VITAL LOOSE SCHOOL TARTAR
Answer: What the discount real estate broker offered to sell—"LOTS" FOR LITTLE

28. **Jumbles:** TUNED NUDGE BOILED POTTER
Answer: That door-to-door salesman got only one order—"GET OUT!"

29. **Jumbles:** ARRAY GAWKY COBALT INWARD
Answer: What an absconder steals after he steals money—AWAY

30. **Jumbles:** OUNCE ABHOR FELONY NAUSEA
Answer: He laughed up his sleeve because that's where this was—HIS FUNNY BONE

31. **Jumbles:** BLESS WHEEL LAYOFF SEETHE
Answer: Why business is always good for the vendor of peanuts—THEY "SHELL" FAST

32. **Jumbles:** FABLE MONEY HERESY SHEKEL
Answer: What a foot doctor sometimes does—HEALS "HEELS"

33. **Jumbles:** KNAVE HEFTY MADMAN BRANDY
Answer: What that canine pair did when Noah's ark came to the end of its voyage—"DE-BARKED"

34. **Jumbles:** DEITY QUAKE WISDOM SLOGAN
Answer: When the authorities caught up with the crooked used car dealer, they took this—THE WIND OUT OF HIS "SALES"

35. **Jumbles:** AWARD ENTRY UNWISE PLOWED
Answer: "Does fish disagree with your wife?"—"IT WOULDN'T DARE!"

36. **Jumbles:** EVENT QUAIL LAXITY STIGMA
Answer: What the diplomats who were attending that important funeral were also doing—"LYING" IN STATE

37. **Jumbles:** FEWER TOOTH SCROLL MARKUP
Answer: How he felt when he flunked the telegrapher's test—"RE-MORSE-FUL"

38. **Jumbles:** PLUME KNOWN HEARTH EFFIGY
Answer: He was always "breaking into" song until he found this—THE RIGHT KEY

39. **Jumbles:** LITHE ARBOR BEHIND OUTING
Answer: Where are some of those yuppies running?—INTO DEBT

40. **Jumbles:** CREEK ALBUM SHERRY MIDWAY
Answer: What the beekeeper said on an unusually hot day—IT'S "SWARM" HERE

41. **Jumbles:** STEED HARPY WHENCE BEFOUL
Answer: What the sign on the door of opportunity reads—"PUSH"

42. **Jumbles:** GAILY SWISH GRAVEN CALIPH
Answer: They resided on the roof because they loved this—"HIGH LIVING"

43. **Jumbles:** HAVEN NATAL ALBINO ELDEST
Answer: That unconvincing witness was making the jury wonder—WHAT "LIES" AHEAD

44. **Jumbles:** ELOPE LIBEL FILLET BUTANE
Answer: What you wouldn't expect a vegetarian to do when the food is unsatisfactory—BEEF ABOUT IT

45. **Jumbles:** APRON FUROR CUDDLE BECALM
Answer: What the quarreling acting team always did just before going on stage—"MADE UP"

46. **Jumbles:** FAVOR BISON WHOLLY MAGNUM
Answer: What that bashful wallflower was hoping to do with the man of her choice—GROW ON HIM

47. **Jumbles:** ELATE CIVIL TUMULT DETAIN
Answer: What a siesta is—A MATINEE "IDLE"

48. **Jumbles:** OPIUM GLOAT DINGHY COBALT
Answer: A guy who tries to start a business on a shoestring sometimes ends up taking this—A GOOD "LACING"

49. **Jumbles:** EXACT CREEL ASSURE POLICY
Answer: The most brutal part of that heavyweight fight—THE PRICE OF THE SEATS

50. **Jumbles:** PENCE VIGIL GIBLET EVOLVE
Answer: The hardest thing to give is—TO GIVE IN

51. **Jumbles:** ADAGE EMERY SLEEPY MUSTER
Answer: What that wild animal trainer at the circus does—"TAMES" TO PLEASE

52. **Jumbles:** ELITE HEDGE LAWFUL THROAT
Answer: That letter made ill will—THE LETTER W

53. **Jumbles:** VAPOR ENJOY JAGGED BOYISH
Answer: What to say when your friendly skeleton leaves on vacation—"BONE VOYAGE"

54. **Jumbles:** ANNOY WHOSE TOFFEE MALTED
Answer: How that tightwad saved money, even on his honeymoon—HE WENT ALONE

55. **Jumbles:** OLDER MINOR ADDUCE FINALE
Answer: What's the best dish to get at a "greasy spoon" restaurant?—A CLEAN ONE

56. **Jumbles:** DOUBT FRUIT JETSAM HAGGLE
Answer: What many "old saws" have done—LOST THEIR TEETH

57. **Jumbles:** LOUSE WEIGH SYSTEM IGUANA
Answer: Some guys are wise, and some are this—"WISE GUYS"

58. **Jumbles:** ANNUL LIBEL ZIGZAG SULTRY
Answer: What the bee got when he tried to phone home—THE "BUZZY" SIGNAL

59. **Jumbles:** GULCH HUMID FRIEZE SINGLE
Answer: The soprano stood on the balcony so she could do this—SING "HIGHER"

60. **Jumbles:** FIFTY GROUP INNING VERIFY
Answer: He's always forgetting, but never this—"FOR GIVING"

61. **Jumbles:** COMET GUILT SUNDAE EFFACE
Answer: What he finally learned how to do while lying on the psychiatrist's couch—STAND ON HIS OWN FEET

62. **Jumbles:** ALIAS EMBER LOCALE SUCKLE
Answer: How much did a belt used to cost?—LESS THAN A "BUCK-LE"

63. **Jumbles:** BLAZE CLOAK LUNACY PACKET
Answer: What it takes to have no eyebrows—A LOT OF PLUCK

64. **Jumbles:** EMPTY DAISY BODICE VIRILE
Answer: Their relative who was known for his stinginess must have been this—VERY "CLOSE"

65. **Jumbles:** UNWED ESSAY JABBER UNSEAT
Answer: What happened when there was a squabble among the astronauts?—THEY SAW STARS

66. **Jumbles:** JOKER DOWNY COWARD HAZING
Answer: The gossip was putting "who" and "who" together and got this—"WHEW!"

67. **Jumbles:** GAUGE CABLE GRUBBY BIGAMY
Answer: What those big-spending tourists returned with—"BRAG" & BAGGAGE

68. **Jumbles:** HOBBY BRAND LIMBER TETHER
Answer: What that famous writer found most absorbing—A BLOTTER

69. **Jumbles:** EXILE HANDY PILFER DEPICT
Answer: What those Stone Age people became when that prehistoric monster suddenly appeared out of nowhere—"PETRIFIED"

70. **Jumbles:** SHOWY AGING WAITER BEHEAD
Answer: What that gum-chewing gambler lost—A BIG WAD

71. **Jumbles:** HAZEL DRAWL FROLIC INFECT
Answer: What was the story about the dog that chased the stick for two miles?—"FAR FETCHED"

72. **Jumbles:** EVOKE MOUNT NEWEST OUTFIT
Answer: What kind of music did the fiddler's squeaking shoes make?—"FOOT NOTES"

73. **Jumbles:** BROIL OUNCE BENUMB STURDY
Answer: The kangaroo proved to be a valuable member of the football team because he was never this—OUT OF BOUNDS

74. **Jumbles:** RAJAH VISOR ANKLET INDIGO
Answer: Provides the main course on a flight—THE NAVIGATOR

75. **Jumbles:** DRAFT PAYEE WOEFUL ACCORD
Answer: The swimming pool was more than he could afford, and now he's—IN DEEP WATER

76. **Jumbles:** PROBE DELVE ADJOIN MUTTON
Answer: She'll no longer stand for being painted—A TIRED MODEL

77. **Jumbles:** FLOUT ELUDE ABSORB WEAPON
Answer: The best place to keep your weight down—BELOW THE BELT

78. **Jumbles:** GAMUT KNELL DECENT LOUNGE
Answer: What word formed in his mind from contemplating that "neat leg"—"ELEGANT"

79. **Jumbles:** KHAKI PORGY JOCKEY TOWARD
Answer: What kids never play in school—HOOKY

80. **Jumbles:** BULGY HENNA ABDUCT ENDURE
Answer: Very commonly causes work stoppages—LUNCH

81. **Jumbles:** WOOZY LASSO EXHALE HARBOR
Answer: With so many owls in the same place, it was hard to tell—WHO'S "HOO"

82. **Jumbles:** RUMMY BLUNT SPRING CENSUS
Answer: To teach addition to the students, the teacher wrote—"SUM" NUMBERS

83. **Jumbles:** WEARY ANKLE FONDUE FRIGHT
Answer: People thought the twins were identical, but their mom—KNEW DIFFERENT

84. **Jumbles:** OBESE CAGEY UNCORK STODGY
Answer: When Brian, Dennis and Carl Wilson roughhoused on the beach, they were being—"BOYS-TEROUS"

85. **Jumbles:** OZONE SNACK BUTANE EXODUS
Answer: The first positive number had a big ego and was proud to be—SECOND TO NONE

86. **Jumbles:** MOVIE LIMIT TANDEM WALNUT
Answer: Mother nature would finish dampening the morning lawns,—ALL IN "DEW" TIME

87. **Jumbles:** THUMP COLIC UNWISE PACKET
Answer: When there weren't enough business-class seats, the baseball player said—PUT ME IN COACH

88. **Jumbles:** COMIC CHUNK SWAMPY DUPLEX
Answer: They were carefully selecting which berries to eat. It was fun to—PICK AND "CHEWS"

89. **Jumbles:** UNCLE CROSS TRENDY LOCALE
Answer: The golfers at St. Andrews decided to extend their trip so they could—STAY THE COURSE

90. **Jumbles:** BLAND AUDIO TOOTHY SPIGOT
Answer: He bought the shirt at the concert 30 years ago. To him it was an—"OLD-T" BUT A "GOOD-T"

91. **Jumbles:** HEAVY MIMIC HYMNAL BUDGET
Answer: The arrogant king who could say "hello" in many languages was—"HI" AND MIGHTY

92. **Jumbles:** SNIFF BUGGY METRIC FIBULA
Answer: It took him a year to lose 100 pounds, which resulted in a—BIG FAT GRIN

93. Jumbles: ROVER AHEAD HECTIC INCOME
Answer: The company was growing quickly, so the number of employees needed to go—"HIRE" AND "HIRE"

94. Jumbles: UPEND ONION HUBCAP METHOD
Answer: The winner of the dog bone eating contest was the—"CHOMPION"

95. Jumbles: TEMPT TIGER HOOPLA LOOSEN
Answer: Napoleon really thought he could win at Waterloo, but he came up—A LITTLE SHORT

96. Jumbles: SPELL TASTY SUBDUE WINERY
Answer: The scuba divers got married underwater and began their new life together in—"WETTED" BLISS

97. Jumbles: INEPT GUIDE BETTOR TOWARD
Answer: If the newspaper reporter was going to turn in the story in time, he'd need to—GET "WRITE" ON IT

98. Jumbles: PERKY WRING LONGER SONATA
Answer: When the tennis players talked business during their match, they were—NETWORKING

99. Jumbles: EIGHT COVER SHRANK CATNIP
Answer: When the chick was ready to leave its shell, it took the—ESCAPE HATCH

100. Jumbles: LOCAL MERGE SPRUNG NIBBLE
Answer: Her very basic approach to teaching students about the human skeleton was—BARE-BONES

101. Jumbles: PIXEL RIVER FEWEST NONFAT
Answer: They had the police artist's silhouette sketch and looked for someone who—FIT THE PROFILE

102. Jumbles: JIFFY MOUTH MIRROR SPRUCE
Answer: Ancient Romans wanted a large public square, so they built a—FORUM FOR 'EM

103. Jumbles: MUNCH PEACE HAGGLE AVATAR
Answer: For sports fans, the invention of the remote control was a—GAME CHANGER

104. Jumbles: LYRIC MESSY VORTEX AUTUMN
Answer: Ben Franklin was able to invent bifocals because of his ability to—"VISUAL-EYES"

105. Jumbles: GOING FOGGY GRUBBY FUTURE
Answer: The dog with the flea problem told the small parasitic insects to—BUG OFF

106. Jumbles: OLDER KNOCK FOSSIL ACCENT
Answer: The first positive odd number considered itself to be—ONE OF A KIND

107. Jumbles: ABOVE SWISH PELLET STURDY
Answer: She called about her unusually high electric bill and asked—"WATTS" UP?

108. Jumbles: DIGIT DRIFT EXEMPT OBJECT
Answer: Getting ready to put on his best suit, he couldn't find his neckwear. He was—FIT TO BE TIED

109. Jumbles: GULCH KNELT PETITE BEWARE
Answer: They successfully drilled for water, and it helped with everyone's—WELL-BEING THERE

110. Jumbles: TWICE KNEED THEORY NUMBER
Answer: Their poker buddy tried to bluff, but they—KNEW "BETTOR"

111. Jumbles: UNITY BEIGE FIDDLE GLITZY
Answer: He had no proof that the food was giving him indigestion, but he did have a—GUT FEELING

112. Jumbles: OMEGA IRONY JOGGER IDIOCY
Answer: James wrote novels such as "Dubliners" and "Ulysses," and his readers—"RE-JOYCED"

113. Jumbles: CLUNG HOARD SPLICE SKIING
Answer: The accountant forgot to add the last number on the page and sat there—NONPLUSSED

114. Jumbles: HOTLY TAKEN ROTATE INWARD
Answer: They had returned, and everyone agreed that the Apollo 11 astronauts were—DOWN TO EARTH

115. Jumbles: FLUSH FROWN MOTION ITALIC
Answer: The caulk and putty guy was out, but there was someone else who could—FILL IN FOR HIM

116. Jumbles: YEAST FLIRT UNPACK VELVET
Answer: The player worked with the tennis instructor in an attempt to fix her—FAULTY SERVE

117. Jumbles: VILLA LIGHT ENOUGH CAMPUS
Answer: They wanted a better view of the small inlet from their home, so they built an—ALCOVE

118. Jumbles: WATCH HASTY MOSAIC TACKLE
Answer: The osprey artist created original paintings and planned to—HAWK THEM

119. Jumbles: VIDEO DROLL MUDDLE TRAUMA
Answer: She thought she came from a large family, but it's—ALL RELATIVE

120. Jumbles: BLURT KITTY FINALE HIDDEN
Answer: When Microsoft co-founder Mr. Gates bought a new suit, he chose one that—FIT THE BILL

121. Jumbles: CARRY DOUSE OUTING LONELY
Answer: The subway train operator was in charge and had everything—UNDER CONTROL

122. Jumbles: EXUDE FLOSS LOTION CANNED
Answer: When he ran over the tire spikes, his front tires lost air in—ONE SECOND FLAT

123. Jumbles: GLADE PRONG CASHEW EYEFUL
Answer: The beachgoers didn't appreciate the seagulls' obnoxiously loud and—"FOWL" LANGUAGE

124. Jumbles: MILKY OUNCE ABRUPT GRASSY
Answer: He was having pain in his lumbar region, and the chiropractor wanted the—BACKSTORY

125. Jumbles: FABLE OFFER VACUUM SHRUNK
Answer: The town's landfill was over capacity and beginning to—"REEK" HAVOC

126. Jumbles: CREST KNACK YONDER STEREO
Answer: After so many successful launches, SpaceX revenue was beginning to—SKYROCKET

127. Jumbles: GRILL TRUNK NOBODY BRIGHT
Answer: The interrupting ram was being rude. They didn't appreciate him—BUTTING IN

128. Jumbles: LUCKY ROUND VIOLET THRIVE
Answer: When the racehorse got off to such a great start right out of the gate, it—LED TO VICTORY

129. Jumbles: WITTY BOXER ENGINE SEASON
Answer: The price of the antique marble bookends was—SET IN STONE

130. Jumbles: POUND BOGUS RANCID JUNGLE
Answer: He would be happy to start work as their new night watchman after—SECURING THE JOB

131. Jumbles: RATIO FUDGE SOCKET LUNACY
Answer: When Gideon Sundback showed how his new zipper worked, people were—"FASTEN-ATED"

132. Jumbles: BIRCH CHURN NAPKIN JAGUAR
Answer: Most of the bats were flying out of the cave, but a few decided to—HANG BACK

133. Jumbles: METAL ALIAS THIRST JUNIOR
Answer: Even when the twins misbehaved, she loved them—JUST THE SAME

134. Jumbles: THREW EAGLE INHALE DIVINE
Answer: To see who was the best arm wrestler, they—HELD AN EVENT

135. Jumbles: FRAME FRANK OUTFIT EMERGE
Answer: The no-cost family photo coupons were—FREE FOR THE TAKING

136. Jumbles: KIOSK RUNNY MEEKLY CACTUS
Answer: During the California Gold Rush, this land owner had a—ONE-TRACK "MINE"

137. **Jumbles:** AGILE HOARD FERRET DOCKET
Answer: The artist initially struggled to learn how to create metal sculptures, but she—FORGED AHEAD

138. **Jumbles:** BURLY ADAPT JUSTLY DOMINO
Answer: The horror movie set in the cemetery had a—BURIAL PLOT

139. **Jumbles:** DITTO EVENT BOUGHT CEMENT
Answer: Because the abacus was old and falling apart, it couldn't—BE COUNTED ON

140. **Jumbles:** SHYLY MODEM HARBOR INFAMY
Answer: They distributed the hospital attendants' new uniforms in an—ORDERLY FASHION

141. **Jumbles:** HONOR ETHIC GENTLE CALMLY
Answer: They discussed reticulated pythons and anacondas—AT LENGTH

142. **Jumbles:** OPERA KNACK CRUNCH DILUTE
Answer: Pickups were introduced in the 1920s. Since then, people have been able to—KEEP ON TRUCKIN'

143. **Jumbles:** COUCH SINGE AVIARY OUTLAW
Answer: After she learned to consistently tie her own shoes,—IT WAS A CINCH

144. **Jumbles:** CLOTH LEAKY SPEEDY LOUNGE
Answer: Elvis Presley's 1957 hit song had some people—ALL SHOOK UP

145. **Jumbles:** DRESS SWUNG MILDEW CATCHY
Answer: When they visited Arizona's famous canyon, the family had a—GRAND TIME

146. **Jumbles:** COCOA KNIFE LITTLE DEFUSE
Answer: When Alfred Hitchcock's movie, "The Birds," premiered in 1963, people—FLOCKED TO IT

147. **Jumbles:** MINCE STYLE SPIRAL CANOPY
Answer: Making Nov. 11 an official holiday to honor veterans was a great idea—IN MANY RESPECTS

148. **Jumbles:** OMEGA WHEAT MINION GLITCH
Answer: The lack of success with his diet was—WEIGHING ON HIM

149. **Jumbles:** DEITY SLANT CANARY QUIVER
Answer: After Apollo 11 touched down on the moon, the astronauts could—"SEA" TRANQUILITY

150. **Jumbles:** QUOTA FLUSH STIGMA MINGLE
Answer: The carpenter shopped for a new hammer that would be—TOUGH AS NAILS

151. **Jumbles:** LOUSY DRILL BEAUTY PLEDGE
Answer: When Broom-Hilda's magic backfired, it—SPELLED TROUBLE

152. **Jumbles:** WEARY DRAFT MISHAP GLOOMY
Answer: Val was silent when Holly called her by her first name, even though—"MOM'S" THE WORD

153. **Jumbles:** STUNT BRAND GIGGLE BOTHER
Answer: When it comes to karate, Chuck Norris has numerous accomplishments—UNDER HIS BELT

154. **Jumbles:** VERGE CATCH SUNSET INDOOR
Answer: The conversation between the architect and general contractor was—CONSTRUCTIVE

155. **Jumbles:** ROBOT YIELD SPRING AWAKEN
Answer: Before they chose a route to travel, they looked at the map to—"WAY" THEIR OPTIONS

156. **Jumbles:** FLEET PLUNK BELLOW LAWYER
Answer: When it comes to Thanksgiving turkey, he tended to eat a lot, which he—KNEW FULL WELL

157. **Jumbles:** EMCEE OCTET CALLUS BRONCO
Answer: The young musician couldn't get the high notes just right and found them—"TREBLE-SOME"

158. **Jumbles:** FAULT LOFTY STYLUS IMMUNE
Answer: They thoroughly enjoyed the flavors of their food in a restaurant that was decorated—TASTEFULLY

159. **Jumbles:** TRULY BLESS SPRAWL BORDER
Answer: The process of an infant becoming a toddler involves—BABY STEPS

160. **Jumbles:** BLEAK DODGE GLOSSY ATTACH
Answer: With every unit rented, the owners of the apartment building were happy,—TO SAY THE "LEASED"

161. **Jumbles:** BRIDGE EYELET CARNAL BEAVER CAUCUS TIPTOE
Answer: The miser's favorite salad—LETTUCE & CABBAGE

162. **Jumbles:** MIDWAY INVOKE THRASH OPENLY RENEGE INTAKE
Answer: What the bartender said that caused the martini drinker to think of Dickens—"OLIVE OR TWIST?"

163. **Jumbles:** NESTLE CAUGHT TEACUP ENGULF OUTCRY AVOWAL
Answer: Possibly his male offspring at the recital—"SON-AT-A" CONCERT

164. **Jumbles:** CHERUB BURLAP CHARGE BUNION CONVEX OUTING
Answer: What the psychiatrist's crabby patient was—A GROUCH ON A COUCH

165. **Jumbles:** PULPIT MARLIN CASKET WHINNY GATHER APATHY
Answer: He makes a nice living without doing a day's work—A NIGHT WATCHMAN

166. **Jumbles:** VALISE NOODLE VANITY WISELY BUNKER DENTAL
Answer: "Do you serve crabs here?"—"WE SERVE ANYBODY"

167. **Jumbles:** DEPICT BLAZER HELPER DISARM EULOGY GENTLE
Answer: This food item can't be beat!—A HARD-BOILED EGG

168. **Jumbles:** ASTRAY GYRATE RECTOR LIKELY AMAZON INLAID
Answer: Who was that famous Indian looking for in the bank?—THE "LOAN ARRANGER"

169. **Jumbles:** ACTING CONVOY EXPOSE METRIC ENMITY NOVICE
Answer: Leaving the neighborhood proved to be this—A "MOVING" EXPERIENCE

170. **Jumbles:** GUIDED CHISEL PRAYER INJECT CANDID FIESTA
Answer: How did the astronaut like his eggs?—STRAIGHT UP

171. **Jumbles:** HAZARD SYRUPY TRIPLE NATIVE BEAKER FELLOW
Answer: He'd passed out while shopping, and they didn't have the—FAINTEST IDEA WHY

172. **Jumbles:** GOALIE FORMAT BLEACH SQUAWK CANNON FEMALE
Answer: She'd just won the racquetball tournament and was—BOUNCING OFF THE WALLS

173. **Jumbles:** MEADOW BITTEN GROUCH GAZEBO PERSON THRIFT
Answer: After Microsoft launched Windows, it didn't take long for people to—GET WITH THE PROGRAM

174. **Jumbles:** DRAGON WALRUS LOOSEN SYSTEM GLOOMY FOSSIL
Answer: The Scrabble player was down by more than 200 points and—AT A LOSS FOR WORDS

175. **Jumbles:** TOMATO CANDID HIGHLY GYRATE ELDEST DELUGE
Answer: Everyone knew Sleepy Hollow's infamous horseman, but he didn't—LET IT GO TO HIS HEAD

176. **Jumbles:** ONWARD HOTTER LEVITY PRANCE FURROW OUTLAW
Answer: The first time the new judo technique was used on him, he was—THROWN FOR A LOOP

177. **Jumbles:** SAVORY DEFEAT MEMOIR MALLET INVEST PUFFIN
Answer: When it came to #1 songs in 1964, the Beatles were—FIRST AND "FOUR-MOST"

178. **Jumbles:** SALMON UNHOOK LOCALE PADDED CLEVER BUSHEL
Answer: They ended the concert just before the storm hit, and the audience left with—RECKLESS "A-BAND-DONE"

179. **Jumbles:** LUNACY MATTER PALACE TAWDRY WALLOP HUDDLE
Answer: Defrosting the turkey days before Thanksgiving was a—WELL "THAWED"-OUT PLAN

180. **Jumbles:** FORMAL GURNEY FOURTH COGNAC SUPERB DEFACE
Answer: When Elon Musk founded SpaceX in 2002, he—LAUNCHED A COMPANY